Translating the Testament of God

A plea for the promotion of Bible translation and language development in Africa.

Translating the Testament of God

A plea for the promotion of Bible translation and language development in Africa.

Napo Poidi

Copyright © 2014–2016 Napo Poidi

Published in 2016 by Wide Margin,
90 Sandyleaze, Gloucester, GL2 0PX, UK
http://www.wide-margin.co.uk/

References to the Biblical text are taken from the RNIV 2011 unless otherwise stated.

The right of Napo Poidi to be identified as the Author of this Work has been asserted by him in accordance with the Copyright, Designs and Patents Act 1988.

All rights reserved. No part of this publication may be reproduced, stored in a retrieval system, or transmitted in any form or by any means electronic, or mechanical, photocopying, recording or otherwise, without the prior permission of the publisher or a licence permitting restricted copying.

ISBN 978-1-908860-17-0

Printed and bound in Great Britain by Lightning Source, Milton Keynes

Contents

Foreword		ix
1	Wycliffe in Africa	1
2	God speaks my language!	23
3	The Bible translation movement in Togo	47
4	An open door for a new translation project	83
5	The birth of Wycliffe-Togo	97
6	Bible translation today and tomorrow	127
7	Epilogue	149

*To all Bible translators
and promoters of language development*

Acknowledgements

I want to recognise and thank all our friends, family and partners for their unfailing support for us in the ministry of Bible translation to which we have been committed for more than thirty years. My thanks also go to the Assemblies of God in Togo, who assigned us to the mission field for Bible translation at a time when this ministry had barely been recognised in Togo.

I am indebted to Mrs. Honorine Gblem-Poidi, my dear wife, linguistics consultant and research lecturer at the University of Lomé, for her very valuable advice and her support during the writing of this book. I am also indebted to Ms. Sheila Crunden, translation consultant, for translating this book into English.

My gratitude and thanks go to everyone, including those whose names have not been mentioned, for their direct or indirect participation in the mission of Bible translation in Togo and in Africa.

Because you have sown with all your hearts, you will reap a harvest of joy on the day when our Lord and Saviour Jesus Christ returns!

To Almighty God alone be the glory!

Foreword

God is doing a new thing

One morning in 1978, a linguist and translator from the mission Wycliffe- Switzerland came to a meeting of the University Christian Union at the Sailors' Home in Lomé, Togo. He came to talk about his passion for the translation of the Bible into local languages, people's mother tongues, and the importance of this for the growth of the church. His message aroused in me a special interest for the translation of the Bible into my mother tongue, Bassar. I realised that the Lord wanted me to give myself to this ministry for the benefit of the 200,000 speakers of the Bassar language. He gave me this verse: "Consider now, for the LORD has chosen you to build a house as the sanctuary. Be strong and do the work." (I Chronicles 28:10)

In 1990, the translation of the New Testament into Bassar was completed. The translation of the Old Testament into that language was begun in 1997 and finished 15 years later. At the same time, the translation of the New Testament into the Igo language was begun in 1991 and completed in 2013.

After the dedication of the New Testament in Bassar in 1992, sharing the vision for the translation of the Bible with the Togolese Church led to the birth in April 2000 of the Wycliffe-Togo Mission for the Translation of the Bible and for Literacy.

God is doing a new thing! He says in the book of the prophet Isaiah 43 v.19:

> "See, I am doing a new thing! Now it springs up;
> do you not perceive it?
> I am making a way in the wilderness and streams
> in the wasteland."

God is in fact doing a new thing for his Church, similar to what he did in the past to save the people of Israel. But the question is the same for us as the one which God asked of the people of Israel through the prophet Isaiah: "Do you not perceive it?" Unless we learn to align our spiritual understanding to what God says, we will not recognise the new thing which God is doing around us today. God can tell us when we must act and when we must wait, when we must stand up and when we must sit down. The Word of God says:

> "Whether you turn to the right or to the left, your
> ears will hear a voice behind you, saying, 'This is
> the way; walk in it.'" (Isaiah 30:21)

In spite of all that we hear around us, we must keep our faith in what God says in the Bible, His Testament for every human. This is how we will be able to understand the implications of what is written in it. John Wycliffe, translator of the Bible into the English of his day and forerunner of the Reformation of the Church in the 14th century, said: "To ignore the Scriptures is to ignore Christ." The Epistle to the

Hebrews tells us about certain Christians who, after having made progress in their knowledge of the Lord, did not see the need to go to their meetings any more, the only means they had to listen to the Scriptures being read. At that time, the Bible was not available for everybody, because printing had not yet been invented. It is not certain if each church had its own scroll, even of some of the books of the Old Testament. This is the reason for the warning given to them: "...not giving up meeting together, as some are in the habit of doing..." (Hebrews 10:25a)

Their ignorance of the Scriptures had caused their love for the Lord to grow cold, because they had forgotten the Biblical truths which previously they had known so well. This had caused them to go backwards in their faith in Christ, and they needed to be taught again the rudiments of God's Word.

> "In fact, though by this time you ought to be teachers, you need someone to teach you the elementary truths of God's word all over again. You need milk, not solid food! Anyone who lives on milk, being still an infant, is not acquainted with the teaching about righteousness." (Hebrews 5:12-13).

Isn't this the risk we all run? "We must pay the most careful attention, therefore, to what we have heard, so that we do not drift away." (Hebrews 2:1).

But can we not say the same about the condition of many Christians in Africa today who have never had access to the Holy Scriptures and so make no effort to find out what they say? In fact, many of them, since their new birth, have not known anything but the milk of the Word of God as it is preached. They have never had access to solid food, because they have never had the opportunity to read the Scriptures for themselves in the language they understand best. No one has taught them to read the Bible, even when it has been translated into their mother tongue. Regular reading of the Bible to the faithful members of the Church is no longer a common practice in all of the meetings or parishes today, because everyone can easily buy their own copy at a very low price. But the Christian who is content with a Christianity which is limited to the forgiveness of sins will not fill his soul with the knowledge of the Word of God. Only the Scriptures, inspired by the Holy Spirit, can make Christians spiritually wise, and enable them to break with traditional beliefs and live by faith in the Word of Christ.

The new thing which God is doing in the mission of Bible translation and literacy in the mother tongues of Africa is a call to the African Church to take on board its responsibilities. The local Church in Africa must consider how it is situated in its own context and in the context of the world today. It ought to be able to organise itself to generate the resources needed for the translation of the Bible, and to train Christians to use the Scriptures translated into each of their mother tongues. Different groups of Christians in Africa should work together, and with their links to Christians in other continents, form a united front for the Mission of God to the world, and in particular for the translation and diffusion of the Testament of God, that is, the Bible, to all the people groups who do not yet have it in their mother tongue.

> *"For this reason Christ is the one who arranges a new covenant, so that those who have been called by God may receive the eternal blessings that God has promised. This can be done because there has been a*

death which sets people free from the wrongs they did while the first covenant was in force." (Hebrews 9:15 TEV)

Chapter 1

Wycliffe in Africa

In his own country, everyone called him 'Mr Wycliffe', but his real name was John Agamah. Mr. Agamah was a retired police officer in Ghana, and he was responsible for communications in the Ghanaian organisation for Bible translation and literacy, called GILLBT (Ghana Institute of Linguistics, Literacy and Bible Translation).

While he was studying in England in the 1950s, Mr. Agamah was invited to teach Ewe, his mother tongue, to missionary translators taking linguistic training at the Wycliffe Centre. He was intrigued by the vision of these young missionaries who were preparing to go to Latin America to translate the Scriptures into the languages of that continent. He began to think about his own country, Ghana, with its many languages which did not yet have an alphabet or a translation of the Bible, as his own language Ewe had.

In fact, German missionaries from the Bremen Mission had already translated the Bible into the Ewe language at the beginning of the 20th century, so Mr. Agamah had been able from a young age to experience the blessing of reading the Bible in his own language. This is why he was concerned about the needs of people who were neighbours of his own Ewe people but who did not have the Scriptures in their own languages. Because of this, he made an urgent appeal to the translators of the Wycliffe Mission to come and translate the Bible into the other languages of Ghana. A few years later, the first Wycliffe missionaries set foot on Ghanaian territory under the auspices of SIL (Summer Institute of Linguistics). This was at the beginning of the 1960s. The mission of SIL in Africa started in Ghana, under the leadership of the pioneers of the work, Dr. George Cowan and Dr. John Bendor-Samuel, who was the first Director of the work of SIL in Africa.

SIL is an international organisation engaged in the development of languages and translation among minority language groups throughout the world. SIL International is the primary partner of the Wycliffe Global Alliance. The two organisations have the same founder, William Cameron Townsend.[1]

In 1936, William Cameron Townsend and his colleagues founded an organisation with the dual purpose of supporting the ministry in which they were engaged among the minority language groups of Mexico, and of recruiting, training and sending people who were called to do the same work that they were doing. They opened a centre for linguistic training in Arkansas in the US. The centre only operated during the summer, hence the name given to the organisation which emerged: 'Summer Institute of Linguistics' (SIL).

The work grew very quickly. In 1942 there were more than a hundred members working on about thirty languages in

[1] William Cameron Townsend and S. Richard Pittman (1974, 1996). *Thou Shalt Remember All The Way*. Dallas, TX: Summer Institute of Linguistics, Inc

Mexico. Gradually, the work expanded into other countries in Latin America, such as Guatemala, Peru and Ecuador. Then there was the need to have a home base to mobilise and send resources to the field. William Cameron Townsend and his co-workers founded the mission Wycliffe Bible Translators in 1942.

In the 1950s, the mission Wycliffe Bible Translators spread to other continents, notably Europe. The work of Bible translation also began in the Pacific region, in the Philippines and in Papua New Guinea. But it was only in the 1960s that the work of Bible translation began in some African countries, beginning in Ghana, when the first Wycliffe translators set foot in that country.

The Summer Institute of Linguistics (SIL) began its work in Ghana in 1962 under a cooperative agreement with the Institute of African Studies at the University of Ghana in Legon. Under this umbrella, SIL was given the mandate of promoting the development of the minority languages of Ghana. From 1962 to 1972, SIL operated in Ghana as an Institute of Linguistics. In 1972, it was decided to change the Institute of Linguistics into a national institution recognised legally under the name of GIL (Ghana Institute of Linguistics), a non-profit organisation. In 1980, the name was changed again to GILLBT (Ghana Institute of Linguistics, Literacy and Bible Translation). GILLBT then signed another partnership agreement with SIL International. Under the terms of this agreement, SIL personnel were assigned to GILLBT to carry out programmes for developing Ghanaian languages. GILLBT could then develop its own identity and ethic, but it remained strongly influenced by the vision and objectives of SIL, the mother organisation, to which it was attached.

Just as for GILLBT in Ghana, the work begun in other countries on the African continent would involve nationals with an intense love for their languages and for the translation of the Word of God into these languages. Thanks to their contribution, similar local organisations came into being to promote the work of Bible translation and literacy. Nevertheless, no matter what route was taken in the formation of these organisations, the DNA of SIL was transmitted to all of them. In Africa, they were grouped under the name of National Bible Translation Organisations (NBTOs). So GILLBT was formed in Ghana, NBTT (Nigeria Bible Translation Trust), BTL (Bible Translation and Literacy) in Kenya, CABTAL (Cameroun Association for Bible Translation and Literacy), ANTBA (National Association for Bible Translation and Literacy) in Burkina Faso, ACATBA (Central African Association for Bible Translation and Literacy), and ATALTRAB (Chadian Association for Literacy and Bible Translation).

Each of these organisations was perceived to be the continuation of the missionary work begun by SIL. The first priority was to put the Holy Scriptures into the hands of the people in their mother tongue, beginning with the New Testament, and through this, to promulgate the work of Bible translation and literacy, with the aim of finishing the translation in each of the languages in need of it within this generation. So all means were used to translate and publish the New Testament and also to promote literacy. The results were phenomenal. Many ethnic and linguistic groups received the New Testament duly translated into their language, the language of their hearts. This contribution by SIL was a determining factor in the growth of the Church in Africa.

GILLBT was a typical example. In 30 years[2] of working on languages which had never before been written, 26 languages

---

[2] S. L. Walter, C. L. Jackson, and T. M. Lawson (1992). "GILLBT, 30 Years Ago". In: *Mother Tongue*

received the New Testament. About 36,000 people had become literate in several hundred literacy classes, facilitated by more than 1700 literacy teachers, supervised by 175 literacy specialists.

Compelled by persecution

Unlike GILLBT, the founding of the second National Bible Translation Organisation, in Nigeria, took place in particularly difficult circumstances. In the 1960s, the Cold War between the Soviet bloc on the one hand and the Western bloc on the other was at its height. African countries were courted by each of the two blocs, seeking to bring as many allies as possible into their camps. At the same time, the Biafran war was raging in Nigeria. The government of Nigeria was becoming more and more distrustful of anything foreign within its territory. In 1976, the Nigerian government decreed that all foreign organisations in the country had to have nationals in their ranks. SIL in Nigeria was under great pressure and was not ready to implement this new regulation. SIL felt the full force of this law, and was ordered to leave the country. The Centre at Jos, in the north of the country, which housed the headquarters of SIL, was requisitioned. It was only then that Christians in administrative positions in Nigeria were asked to come to the rescue of what remained of the organisation. Among them was Dr. John Adive, at that time a teacher and researcher at the University. Dr. Adive and his wife Martha were among the first nationals to be involved in translation with the Nigeria Bible Translation Trust (NBTT). He became its first director.

It was in this way, under the pressure of external circumstances, that NBTT took the place of SIL. During this time, a large proportion of SIL personnel in Nigeria went to neighbouring countries, principally to Ghana and Cameroun, to reinforce the SIL presence in these countries. One couple went to Togo to start a new branch of SIL.

This crisis which began in Nigeria would catch up with SIL again in 1979, in Nepal in Asia, where the translators of the Bible were forced to leave the country.

These events made a big contribution to the involvement of nationals in the Bible translation work of SIL in Africa. SIL personnel who had been forced to leave Nigeria felt compelled to change strategy in the new countries they had entered. Certain nationals who had done exceptionally well in the linguistic courses offered by SIL were accepted as members on the same basis as the expatriates. Among them were Joseph Nfonyam in Cameroun, Justin Frempong and Grace Adjekum in Ghana, Napo and Honorine Poidi in Togo, and Barnabé and Eliane Mensah in Benin. Other well-known people such as Emmanuel Ndjok in Cameroun, William Adai in Ghana, Daniel Campaoré in Burkina Faso, Abel Ndjerareou in Chad, also played an important role in the promotion of Bible translation in Africa.

Thereafter, SIL emphasised sharing the vision for Bible translation with the churches, and with the University Christian Unions, where a large number of Christian intellectuals were concentrated, especially in French-speaking countries.

In other countries, notably in Kenya, the experience of GILLBT and NBTT inspired the pioneers of the work of Bible translation. Under the impetus of Micah Amubokole, the church leaders in Kenya adopted another strategy to found the Bible translation movement in Kenya. SIL would not be able to start another 'branch' as they had done in other countries, but rather a 'working group'. The difference was one of size.

A branch needed official recognition and a residence permit in the receiving country. On the other hand, a working group could operate under the cover of a national institution, and could be dissolved easily. Thus the only official institution was Kenyan. The Bible Translation and Literacy organisation (BTL) was founded in Kenya in 1984. The SIL working group in Kenya then signed a cooperative agreement with BTL. This agreement enabled SIL to assign personnel to BTL, but only with BTL's agreement. The local church in Kenya had learnt lessons from the Nigerian experience.

The fourth period in the history of missions

The missiologist Ralph Winter (Winter 1981)[3] divided the history of modern missions into three periods: the first period started with William Carey, the father of modern missions, in 1792; the second with Hudson Taylor in 1865; and the third with William Cameron Townsend in 1917. But today, it is understood that a fourth period began when the receiving countries became independent, when national mission organisations started in the countries which up until then had been the beneficiaries of missionary work. This fourth period began with many challenges, particularly those of developing an equal partnership between western missions and the national missions which started with big financial needs.

This fourth period also inaugurated a new approach to the translation of the Scriptures into minority languages. Up until that time, the translations were made by expatriate missionaries with the help of native speakers who had a low level of education. These native speakers worked with the translation

[3] Ralph Winter is the founder of the US Center for World Mission in Pasadena, California.

teams as language informants, helping the SIL linguists. From now on, the translation of the Bible would be done by native speakers trained in the principles of translation advocated at the beginning of the 1960s by Nida and Taber, two outstanding figures in the world of Bible translation at the time. They taught that the job of the translator was to reproduce in the receptor language the nearest equivalent of the text of the source language. For Nida and Taber, the essential role of the translator was to convey the message in such a way that the reader in the receptor language would have the same experience that the original reader would have had. The form of the text was to be maintained and changed only where it made the meaning of the original text clearer in the receptor language. Only a native speaker who possesses the intuition of his language, and who also knows the principles of translation, is capable of achieving this objective. In this way, the role of the mother tongue translator came to the fore.

Today we are seeing the emergence of a new generation of mother tongue translators who are able to translate directly from the original Hebrew and Greek texts. This turning-point, which aims at excellence in translating the Bible, has been made possible by the vision of people like Halvor and Mirja Ronning who founded the Home for Bible Translators,[4] based at Yad Hashmona on the outskirts of Jerusalem in Israel, which trains translators in Biblical Hebrew. A few years ago I myself benefited from this training.

The involvement of national translators who have been well educated and trained accelerates the work and improves the quality of Bible translation into their mother tongue. The translators into local languages who have been well trained in Israel must be in dialogue with other workers in the local

---

[4] Now known as the Jerusalem Center for Bible Translators (JCBT).

church to encourage discussion and develop Christian thought in Africa. If they do not do that, the African Church will remain dependent on the thinking of the theologians and leaders of Western and Asian churches. On the contrary, the African Church has much to give to the world in its expression of faith in Jesus Christ.

In actual fact, this generation of mother tongue translators who have come out of training in Israel are better equipped to correct errors in Bible translation, some of which were introduced in the early centuries of the church, from the time that the Hebrew Bible was considered part of the Christian canon. Some of these errors stemmed from new interpretations, and the application of levitical terminology to the Church. For example, Malachi 1:10-14 was reinterpreted following a line of thinking according to which the church had replaced Israel ('Replacement Theology'[5]), contrary to the reaffirmation in Romans 9-11 of the status of Israel as the 'chosen people of God'. This reinterpretation resulted in the development of titles like 'priest' instead of 'elder' to indicate the leader of a local church, and the use of 'priesthood' to describe Christian ministry.

Outside of these interpretations, there are also other difficulties linked to the original text from which certain old translations of the Bible were made into European languages. For example, the canonical text of the Hebrew Bible is the traditional one called the Masoretic Text. This version contains clear indications for pronunciation which were made two thousand years ago for the reading of the text in synagogues. This text with its readings was confirmed when archaeologists found manuscripts of the Hebrew Bible at Qumran. These texts

---

[5] Ronald E. Diprose (2004). *Israël dans le développement de la pensée chrétienne.* Saône: La joie de l'Eternel

are called the 'Qumran Scrolls'. These Scrolls are at least two thousand years old, and contain the text of the Bible that was read in the first century in synagogues and probably by Jesus himself. The Scrolls and the ancient Qumran village can be seen in the Land of the Bible, near the Dead Sea in Israel today. The accent marks, called *tehamim* (which means 'spices') give 'flavour' to the text, that is, they indicate the way one should read the text so that the meaning is clear. These accents have been transmitted faithfully from generation to generation by the Masoretes, a group of Jewish scribes who devoted their lives to copying faithfully the Biblical text that has been preserved until today. The *tehamim* give the divisions of the Text and show the relations between the different parts of the Biblical discourse. These *tehamim* are very useful to the alert mother-tongue translator of the Bible when he finds himself faced with a difficult choice to make during the course of his translation. Consider the examples in Isaiah 40:3 and Genesis 10:21:

For Isaiah 40:3, I picked up two versions of the Bible in English. The first one is the well known and respected English version: the *Authorised Version* (AV) or *King James* Bible (KJV). The second is the translation made by Jewish scholars: *The Jewish Publication Society* Bible (JPS). I was reading in the Book of Isaiah 40:3. The two versions were presenting me with two different readings of the same verse. Where is the *"desert"* (*"midbar"* in Hebrew)? According to KJV, the desert is the place from which the voice was calling: "The voice of him that crieth in the wilderness, 'Prepare ye the way of the LORD.'" According to the JPS, the desert is where the path of the Lord is to be made and we don't know where the voice is calling from: 'A voice rings out: "Clear in the desert a road for the LORD."' To me as a translator, it is important to know which reading I should take and on what grounds that decision should be made.

The responsibility of the translator is very obviously apparent here. He is making a translation for the Church and for his people group, a translation that will affect the life and the faith of people in the Church. The two English translations failed to inform him. He is in a dilemma. Knowledge of the Hebrew Bible is then essential. The Hebrew text of the Bible, the Masoretic Text, the "traditional text", provides clear indications of how the text was read two thousand years ago. This text and its readings have been confirmed by the Qumran Scrolls. This finding reaffirms the Biblical truth we have in our hands. The Masoretic Text provides the vocalisation and accentuation of the Text. The reading that the Masoretic Text provides is the one the Jewish Publication Society follows in this verse 3 of Isaiah 40. However, in Matthew 3:3 and John 1:23 we read: 'A voice of one calling in the wilderness, "Prepare the way for the Lord"'. Here the quotation has been taken from another source, the Septuagint, which is a translation of the Hebrew text into Greek.

In Genesis 10:21, before one can translate the verse, one has to decide which of Japheth and his brother is the elder of the two. In most African languages, there is a distinction between older and younger in the kinship terms: there is a difference between 'older brother' and 'younger brother', and also between 'older sister' and 'younger sister'. For the Bassar, the distinction goes further, between the two sexes. So before translating, it is necessary to do a component analysis of the kinship terms. This distinction is not made in European languages, or in Hebrew. Here too, the *tehamim* make the reading in the text clear and so the translation task is facilitated for the mother-tongue translator. There are numerous passages in the Bible where the *tehamim* enable the translator to solve problems by referring to the Hebrew text.

This difficulty in translating kinship terms is also found in the New Testament. For example, consider John 11 and try to translate the first two verses into an African language which makes a distinction between 'younger sister' and 'older sister', or 'older brother' and 'younger brother', and also between 'brother of a female person' and 'sister of a male person'. A back- translation of John 11:1-2 in a language using these kinship terms would be: 'There was a sick man called Lazarus, of Bethany, the village of Mary and Martha, her *elder-sister*. Mary was the one who anointed the Lord with perfume, and wiped his feet with her hair, and it was her *brother of a female person* Lazarus who was sick.'

This shows the importance not only of linguistic and sociolinguistic research, but also knowledge of the original languages of the Bible, the text and contexts of the Bible, before translating the text of the Bible into any language. However, the problem of Bible translation lies in the choices made by the translators. Every translation of the Bible has to answer a fundamental question: Should it bring the Bible to the people, or bring the people to the Bible? In the first case, there is a question of the translation of unknown concepts, that is, of contextualisation. In the second case, the translation gives the speakers of the receptor language a message which was first given to a foreign people in a foreign context (that of the people of Israel), and so not necessarily understood by everyone without interpretation. We have the example of the Ethiopian Eunuch in the Acts of the Apostles, who needed the help of Philip to understand the message he was reading:

> 'The Spirit told Philip, "Go to that chariot and stay near it." Then Philip ran up to the chariot and heard the man reading Isaiah the prophet. "Do you understand what you are reading?" Philip

asked. "How can I," he said, "unless someone explains it to me.'" (Acts 8:29-31).

A dialogue between translators of the Bible, theologians, pastors, evangelists, and other leaders of the local Church is therefore imperative for each ethnic and linguistic group where a translation is in progress or planned in minority languages. In Togo, the following associations are found: ACEB (Bassar), ACATBLI (Ife), OADI (Igo), APSEK (Kabiye), APLA (Akebu), ABTem (Tem), ACPLL (Lama), ASDN (Nawdm), ATAPEB (Moba). In Francophone Africa, the 'Francophone Initiative' (R. Pohor and M. Kenmogne 2012) should offer a suitable framework for this dialogue. Theological reflection in Africa should be based on sound hermeneutical principles, that is, (i) taking account of the whole canon of the Bible properly translated into the local languages, (ii) a recognition of the Jewish nature of Jesus, of the Old Testament and of a large part of the New Testament.

Partnership or Dependency?

The financial crises which have shaken the world, notably since the events of 11th September 2001 in New York in the USA, have revealed the weakness of the model which western missions followed in their partnerships with African missions.

To begin with, the foreign agencies came with pre-planned projects, ready to fund one hundred per cent the various missions and activities of their partners on the mission field. Relationships in this period were based on the idea of the 'offer'. The percentage of available funding began to diminish with the repeated crises in the world. A relationship based on the 'offer' was shown to be limited. The offer from outside was no longer able to take into account all the realities and the specific needs of the beneficiaries. Evaluations showed that the expected results had not always been achieved. This gave birth to another kind of relationship based on 'demand'. At the present time, the proportion of the relationships based on the 'offer' is almost at zero, while the number of relationships based on 'demand' is growing strongly. This shows that the level of participation by the communities who benefit is becoming ever greater, and is indeed essential for the realisation of development projects.

The National Bible Translation Organisations (NBTOs) were no exception. At the beginning of 2000, under the pressure of the systemic financial crisis, all of NBTOs needed a transfusion of financial resources from the outside, particularly from their partners Wycliffe and SIL International. Work in the translation projects was scaled down. Worse still, qualified national personnel in the various domains of the ministry of Bible translation had not been adequately prepared to take over the work. Since the object of the NBTOs was the same as that of SIL, the essential work was to translate the New Testament and make it accessible to the communities who would benefit from it.

Up until that time, there had been very little transfer of competencies to nationals, and no transfer at all to the receptor communities of the responsibility for translating the Bible. This situation put the continuity of the NBTOs outside of the expatriate 'mother mission' into doubt. Worse still, the local church, which had never really been involved in the mission, was considered to have nothing to offer to the work of translating the Bible into their local languages. Her place was reduced to that of someone in need of help; unfortunately, often to her great satisfaction.

In spite of that, the history of Bible translation in Africa demonstrates the important part played in the work by certain well-known figures from the African Church. The Right Reverend Samuel Ajayi Crowther, (c.1809-1891) the first African bishop of the Anglican church in Nigeria, is an example: he began and oversaw to the end the translation of the Bible into Yoruba. Naturally, since the local church has not been particularly involved in the translation of the Bible, we are still waiting to see what lasting impact will come from the use of the finished product in the propagation of the good news of Jesus Christ and the transformation of the lives of the beneficiaries. "For where your treasure is, there will your heart be also." (Luke 12 :34).

The result of all this is that many translations of the New Testament, made at the cost of long years of work and sacrifice, remain closed books for many families. Even years after the euphoria of the dedication of 'God's Book' in the mother tongue, it is not rare to find cases where only a handful of readers take the trouble to open 'the Book'.

Today it is obvious that a change of model is necessary in the context of the modern world. The Church in Africa must realise its duty and become more proactive. The world is constantly changing and becoming more and more complex and interdependent. People are bound together because they have to work together to achieve their goals. Today, no nation can act relying on its own strength alone. Even powerful nations like the USA and Russia can no longer make decisions without paying attention to even the weakest nation.

Long before this, in the middle of the crisis which shook Togo in 1992, a specialist in the African context, Professor Lantam Seyi, declared to a local forum of development workers:

> The new society which is being formed, and which will emerge from the convulsions which are now taking place in Africa, will be characterised principally by a strong disengagement of the State from numerous vital aspects of the life of the community, on the one hand nationally and locally, and on the other by the increasing strength of civil society which will take over public responsibilities.

That is to say, in simple language, that the ordinary citizens, men and women like you and me, individually or collectively in organisations and popular groupings in a voluntary capacity, will be responsible for identifying the personal and collective needs and will freely undertake to do whatever is in their power to satisfy those needs.

In this way, the responsibility for satisfying the individual and collective needs of society will be transferred for the most part to the citizens themselves, at whatever stage they are at. The State, for its part, will henceforth be content to play the role of referee, trainer and supervisor. It will use legal and institutional means to ensure that everyone is equally and properly protected, so that there will be progress in an atmosphere of liberty, peace and security.

It is obvious that this increase in civilian agents will not be resourced by waving a magic wand. On the contrary, a deliberate and careful preparation by committed volunteers will be necessary. It will be the work of men and women who from now on will consecrate themselves and their spiritual, intellectual, material and financial resources for it.

This is the society of the future which is beckoning! The local church must adapt to the changes taking place in her environment, and fully play her part within the different people groups amongst which she has been planted.

The conclusion is obvious: the traditional model of the 'Offer'—a relationship of superior strength and resources which was followed by mission agencies to achieve Bible translation—has come to an end. A new model, more closely related to the local situation and based on 'Demand'—that is to say on the changing relationship of interdependence and interaction—must take its place. Instead of developing a dependency which relies wholly on foreign funds, it is partnership which must be encouraged; first of all within the country itself, to support missions and their missionaries. From now on we must apply this principle conscientiously and effectively; we must stop acting in ways that inhibit the positive effects of the transformation that Bible translation brings to local churches and the people they serve.

This realisation recently caused Wycliffe and SIL to begin a new initiative in Bangladesh ('The Bangladesh Advance') with a view to transforming the nation. The idea is to coordinate strategies which could potentially achieve important results and which are based on giving local populations the responsibility for achieving those results. It was Bengal (from which the modern state of Bangladesh was created in 1971) which received the gospel two hundred years ago, thanks to the ministry of William Carey, the father of modern missions. Nevertheless today, two centuries later, this country which was the cradle of modern missions remains not only one of the countries which is considered unreached by the gospel but also one of the poorest countries in the world. All the missions are in agreement that the transformation of the peoples of Bangladesh will not be achieved in the first instance by foreign initiatives. God has a plan for the local church in this country: it is that she should obey Him by committing herself wholeheartedly to her mission, so that the Spirit can transform communities and the whole nation.

So that a real change can take place, the Church and the local populations must become the agents of transformation by committing themselves to it effectively. It is here that the emergence of the Wycliffe organisations in Africa makes sense. Moreover, the bitter experience caused by the world crisis has aroused the collective conscience of the Church and the nations in Africa that they must first count on their own resources if Africa is to make progress.

Understanding the mission of translating the Bible

The mission of translating the Bible, like every other Christian mission, can be considered 'a participation in the extension of the *Missio Dei* ('God's Mission') in the world'.[6]

In order to better understand Wycliffe's mission for the translation of the Bible, it is important to return to the very beginning; that is, to look again at the context in which God called John Wycliffe in England in 1382 to the mission of translating the Bible into everyday English. The mission of John Wycliffe can be summarised in one sentence which is well-known even today in the history of the Church: 'John Wycliffe, the Morning Star of the Reformation'. The morning star had infiltrated the English local church, and its light had overcome the darkness which had covered this church. The light, that is, the Word of God, had taken its place in the life of the local church over time, because the Bible had been translated into the English spoken at that time, and the reading of it was promoted. There is not a shadow of doubt that William

[6]Citation from the missiologist Karl Hartenstein.

Cameron Townsend was inspired by this when he founded his second organisation in 1942 and called it 'Wycliffe Bible Translators'.

So at the appointed time, God raised up the Wycliffe Bible Translators to make the Word of God shine in all the mother tongues spoken in the Church, and by each ethnic and linguistic community in the world which needed it. But the most important lesson to be learnt is that God always maintains sovereignty over His mission down the ages. Consequently, it is up to us to learn what God wants us to do by a careful analysis of the acts of God.

God acts according to His will in His own time

> "But when the set time had fully come, God sent his Son" (Galatians 4:4)

God acts according to His will in His own time! If we study the context of the period called 'the set time' in Judea, we will discover that certain conditions had come together before God intervened in history. Of these preliminary conditions we will cite two: an unprecedented period of peace in the Mediterranean world imposed by the Roman Empire (the *Pax Romana* of the 1st and 2nd centuries AD), and a favourable linguistic and cultural context. These two conditions were essential for the coming of the Son of God, and the propagation of the Good News which he was to bring to the world.

Concerning this favourable linguistic and cultural context: first of all, the Hebrew language had been established for more than a thousand years. Hebrew had become a definitive language, because it was the expression of the Jewish religion, which also had a definite form. Then God permitted the emergence and subsequent invasion of the linguistic and cultural power of the Greek language into the world of that time. Greek had developed a common language, Koine Greek, which was very well suited to expressing the new knowledge of the time. This Greek language was widely spoken throughout the Mediterranean basin before the time of Christ. The line of demarcation between oral and written literature in Hebrew and in Greek had been crossed, and effective communication was possible in both languages. The translation of the Bible from Hebrew into Greek, the Septuagint, was made two centuries before Christ without difficulty.

In addition, philosophical debates about life and existence were common in the society of that time. Not surprisingly, this cultural development also encouraged the pagan religions of the time. These were well organised and structured, with a focus on life beyond the grave. This explains clearly what is described in the Acts of the Apostles (Acts 17 23-33). In Athens, Paul did not need to perform a miracle to communicate the Gospel to the Greeks. The idea of 'the unknown god', well known to the Greeks of the time, was sufficient to make a bridge to the thinking of the Athenians.

The African context

The situation in Africa today is quite different to the one we have just described.

First of all, traditional religion in Africa is primarily concerned with life here on earth, not life after death; there is no focus on the after-life similar to that held by the Greeks. In Africa, there is normally a recognition of the existence of a supreme being who created the heaven and the earth, but people prefer to seek protection from the gods or the ancestors in order to be assured of well-being on this earth.

Furthermore, the African context is nearer to the Romano-European experience of the period of John Wycliffe in the 14th century. Christianity was running the risk of making a death-leap: bypassing Biblical spirituality and becoming a religion linked to magic, in particular attempts to manipulate events, and in spiritism. But, when religion is confused with magic manipulation, there is grave danger; the Word of God, whose purpose is to bring light, on the contrary becomes obscure, frightening, opaque, and reserved only for the initiated. This is how occultism arises.

At the time, the Bible and the religious services were only in Latin, and this separated the believers from the divinity. The priest, even if he did not replace God, became the only intermediary. In this situation, there are two possible outcomes:

- When the intermediaries have a pecuniary interest, and the desire for profit gains the upper hand, peculiar interpretations of the Holy Scriptures result. This is very much the case for a good number of preachers and pastors in Africa.

- When the intermediaries themselves are ignorant, not having received a revelation themselves, they are forced to stick to the letter in order to show themselves to be honest. Otherwise, it is a spirit of deceit which is substituted for the Spirit of truth, and which proclaims in the name of God things which He has never said.

The dearth of the light of the Word of God, of knowledge and of foresight—in short the lack of Christian thinking undermines the Continent today. The African Church urgently needs to lay proper foundations in its local mother tongues, and train an army of literates in those mother tongues.

The mission of Wycliffe Bible Translators has the privilege of being the forerunner of revival in the local African churches, according to what is written: "Wake up, sleeper, and Christ will shine on you."

Mombasa, Kenya, 1989

With this in view, in September 1989, the leaders representing the NBTOs in Africa, Asia and the Pacific were invited to Mombasa in Kenya, for an orientation workshop lasting one month, under the auspices of David Cummings (the president of Wycliffe International) and Dr. John Bendor-Samuel. The aim was to reshape the vision which had been transmitted to the NBTOs for Bible translation. The focus of the seminar was on the involvement of national Christians in the translation of the Bible. Various other related themes were also discussed, such as relations with the churches and the mobilisation of resources. After this training, the participants were more or less equipped to initiate and develop partnerships with the local churches in their respective countries. Mombasa marked a turning-point in the realisation of the vision for Bible translation in Africa, in the sense that the involvement of the local church was put at the centre of the ministry of translating the Bible into local languages.

Chapter 2

God speaks my language!

The 24th June 1991 will always be a memorable date in the history of Togo. On that day the Conference of National Sovereignty[1] for Togo began in Lome, at the House of Congress. If this conference had not taken place, the country would have been in danger of sliding into the horrors of civil war. Resentment, vengeance and inter-tribal hatred had taken over the country. In some places, the police and customs officers had been driven from their posts by militias, encouraged by the local population. These militias took control of the roads and ill-treated all those who were not of the same language

---

[1] The Conference of National Sovereignty was a round-table which united all the institutions active in the country to look for solutions to the social and political problems of the nation. The first Conference of National Sovereignty was initiated by the lawyer Robert Dossou in the Republic of Benin. In Togo, the agreement made on 12th June between the Opposition and the Party in power paved the way for the opening of the Conference of National Sovereignty.

and ethnic group that they were. The Conference of National Sovereignty brought together nearly all the institutions active in the country for several weeks. One after another, they expressed themselves virulently on the rostrum of the House of Congress (today it is the Parliament building), either to approve or to excoriate the policies of the military regime which had governed the country for three decades. At the end of these debates, the Conference of National Sovereignty defined a new direction for the country's political system and the leaders of the nation. They also put in place the instruments of political transition which led to the very first democratic elections in the history of the country.

But from a spiritual point of view, 24th June 1991 will always be a memorable date because it was on that day that 2000 copies of the first New Testament which had ever been translated into the Bassar (Ncham) language arrived in the port of Lome. It was the first New Testament translated by SIL into a Togolese language. The Bassar people could then shout: "There is not a shadow of doubt about it—God speaks my language!"

Twelve months had passed since this New Testament had been typeset and sent to the printers in South Korea. For a whole year, the churches in Bassar had been concentrating on organising the dedication of 'the Testament of God' in the Bassar language, and its presentation to the Bassar people. The ceremony would take place in the town of Bassar, about 400 km from the capital, Lome. For such a large gathering, it would be prudent to wait until the sociopolitical situation in the country had calmed down. Prayers went up from believers everywhere to beg the Lord God to intervene. No-one had any doubt about the risks of transporting 2000 copies of the New Testament from Lome to Bassar by road. The organisation of a peaceful dedication ceremony was unimaginable in the town of Bassar, which had been the scene of violent clashes between political adversaries. The Bassar people in Togo, and from neighbouring Ghana, would be travelling for this celebration of 'God's Book' in the Ncham language, the symbol of their people's emancipation. The light of the Word of God was at last to hand. The shining light of the Morning Star would penetrate the Bassar people and remove the darkness which covered them. No Bassar Christian would want to miss that unique occasion. God takes pleasure in seeing His people, wherever they are, answering His call and taking part in His work. But it was necessary to wait for the right time to celebrate.

Nevertheless, we should not miss the forest for the trees. The ultimate goal of the translation of the Bible into a language is to see the Holy Scriptures used in the daily life of the people, for their salvation in Christ. One cannot be satisfied only with celebrating a New Testament, or even a whole Bible, in a local language. To arrive at this goal, the local church must take ownership very early on of the translation project, and commit to the diffusion of the finished product. The church is God's primary instrument for the accomplishment of His mission. By involving the local church in the realisation of a translation of the Bible, God creates the conditions necessary for the future spread of the light of His Word in the church and in the language community.

The translation of the Testament of God into the Bassar language: Beginnings in Ghana

It all began in 1962. At that time, the first group of Wycliffe translators arrived in Ghana. In this group were two young women, Sonia Hine and Jocelyn Clevenger. These two translators of the Bible were sent to work on the Ncham language among the Bassar people of Ghana. They went to live in the village of Nkanchina in the Volta Region, where they began to learn the language. But this was only for a short time, because they were replaced by two other young translators, also dedicated to the work. These were Mary Abbott and Monica Cox. They decided to go to live in a different village among the Bassar people in Ghana, called Lungi. They in their turn began to learn the Ncham (Bassar) language there.

In 1962, the first researchers from SIL in Ghana were under contract to the Institute of African Studies of the University of Ghana in Legon (IAS). The IAS had identified eight languages, of which Bassari/Tobote was one, for SIL to research. These researchers had followed two courses in linguistics (equivalent to two years of study at university level), and so were able to begin their study of these languages. Sonia Hine made a list of words and sorted the nouns into classes. In 1963, Mary Abbott made an outline of the phonology and the grammar, while in 1964 Monica Cox began a tonal analysis.

In November 1964, they attended a linguistic research workshop under the leadership of Professor Kenneth L. Pike, and then another workshop for describing the phonology, led by Professor Pike and Pamela Bendor-Samuel. As a result of these two workshops, a publication was produced in the series 'Collected Field Notes'. (Abbott and Monica Cox 1966)

However, the very first studies describing the Bassar language had been made by Dietrich Westermann (1922). He made a word-list and an overview of the Bassar language. Other work was done by Father André Prost (1963). Today there are several other research studies which have been made in Ncham. (Gblem-Poidi and Kantchoa 2012)

The move to Togo

In 1967, Mary and Monica decided to visit Togo, a country neighbouring Ghana, where there is a large Bassar community. They then discovered that it was the country where the Bassar people originated. As a result of their contacts with the National Library and the National Institute for Scientific Research (INRS), they were officially welcomed by the Togolese authorities. They decided to move to Togo, and went to live in the town of Bassar to continue their work of linguistic research and translation of the Bible into the Ncham language. Mary and Monica's move to Togo resulted in the signing of an official agreement in 1975 setting up a branch of SIL in Togo.

The two translators were helped by a pastor who was a native speaker of Bassar, Pastor Gbandi Claude Wagbé. However, not long after their move, Mary Abbott left the team in order to join the translation project in the Konkomba language in Ghana, where she worked with another colleague, Mary Steele. During this time, Monica Cox continued her research which resulted in the publication in 1974 of *La Phonologie du Bassari* (A Phonology of Bassari), and a proposal for the orthography of the Ncham language. This was the fruit of several years of research with her co-workers Tchapo Daré, Pastor Gbandi Claude Wagbé and Labanté Samuel Nabine.

Happily for the Bassar project, in 1969 a new translator, Sheila Crunden, joined the team in Bassar. Sheila worked initially with Tchapo Daré on a primer for a pilot literacy class in the Ncham language, and subsequently on two new primers with another native Bassar speaker, Tchandikou Kpambé. Pastor Claude Wagbé gave way to Labanté Samuel Nabine, who was a tailor by profession. He would work on the translation project part-time from 1969.

From the GBU to Bible translation

In 1978, after the expulsion of SIL personnel from Nigeria, Paul and Inge Meier, translators of the Bible with Wycliffe Switzerland, landed in Togo. This couple came to Togo as SIL administrators and promoters of Bible translation. The bitter experience of their expulsion from Nigeria was a wake-up call for the Meiers that it was essential to share the vision for Bible translation with the educated Christians of a country. That was how the Meiers came to give a talk about translating the Bible at a meeting of the GBU (University Christian Union) in Lomé. I attended in my capacity as General Secretary of the GBU. It was my first exposure to the vision of translating the Bible into people's mother tongues. After this meeting, and reflecting on what I had heard, I realised that God was calling me to the ministry of Bible translation into my own language. I could not resist the call of God. In 1978, I joined Paul and Inge Meier, this pioneer couple of SIL in Togo, and traveled throughout Togo and Benin speaking about the work of SIL, and in particular for the project of translating the New Testament into Bassar.

Overcoming the obstacles to translating the Bible

Up to that time, the linguistic research undertaken on the Bassar, or Ncham, language had resulted in the publication of the basic phonology of the language. Traditional stories had been collected and some portions of the Scriptures had been translated. So part of the New Testament had already been translated into Ncham. There was a need for someone to type the translation, to revise it, and to test the style with other speakers, as well as to complete the translation of the rest of the New Testament. But obstacles were mounting against the completion of this project. Monica Cox had to return to her home in England for health and other reasons. Samuel Nabine had already left the project to follow an advanced course in tailoring in Lomé, the capital of Togo. Sheila Crunden was alone with no co-worker. The project had to be reorganised.

First of all, Samuel Nabine was recalled to the project and a new recruit was needed. Pastor Gnon Bartholomew Nabine joined the team and by the beginning of 1979, the obstacles had at last been overcome. There was a new team of four members to take up the project again: Sheila Crunden, Labanté Samuel Nabine, Pastor Gnon Bartholomew Nabine, and myself.

In the summer of that year, before starting work again, the team went to a training course on translation principles in Yamassoukro in Ivory Coast, and to another on literacy in Ouagadougou in Burkina Faso. Monica Cox had returned from England, but after a year, at the beginning of 1981, she left for good.

In the spring of 1981, the first draft of the translation of the New Testament in the Ncham language was finished. A literacy primer had also been published, thanks to the dedicated work of Sheila, Tchandikou and Tchapo.

Testing the translation

Having translated the New Testament into the Bassar language, we could not put its light under a bushel, but upon a candlestick to shine on the whole people. The testing of the translation for its style with native Ncham speakers provided the opportunity. This testing took place over the period of a year, between 1981 and 1982. Several young Christians, native speakers of the language, undertook this work under my supervision. After training them in the principles of translating and revising the translation of the Bible, I taught them the methods by which the style and quality of a good translation could be tested with the target population, before producing the final version. These translation testers left each day by bicycle to go to different locations in the Bassar area, sometimes as far as 35 km from the town of Bassar, in order to read the Bassar translation of the New Testament to groups of people who had assembled in the home of the village chief.

This stage of testing the translation in Bassar reminds us of the strategy used by John Wycliffe and his team in the 14th century in England. After finishing the translation of the Bible into their mother tongue, the co-workers of John Wycliffe spread out through the counties and villages of their native land to read their translation of the Bible in the English mother tongue to ordinary people. These preacher-evangelists were called 'lollards', because it was said that they 'lolled' or idled away their time. It was a pejorative word, because the 'lollards' went everywhere and talked much about the gospel of Jesus Christ in the common language. Some people called them 'the disciples of Wycliffe'.

The effect on the Church and on the people thirsty to hear the truths of the Bible was immediate. While the ordinary people glorified God for the light of the Word which they heard in the language of their hearts, the clergy sought ways and means to put an end to the ministry of John Wycliffe and his co-workers. The clergy were more concerned to protect the 'sacred book' of which only they, the initiated, guarded the secret.

History tells us that the clergy conspired to persecute ferociously and put to death these forerunners of the Reformation of the Church. The end of John Wycliffe was one of the most dramatic. Even after his death and burial, the persecution of John Wycliffe did not stop. His detractors unearthed his bones, which they burnt, and threw the ashes into the River Swift in England. This river in turn carried the ashes into the Atlantic Ocean. The tragic end of John Wycliffe, who had served the cause of Bible translation in his mother tongue, is a witness to the extent of the commitment necessary for the mission of Wycliffe in translating the Bible for the Church. Today translating the Bible into people's mother tongues has reached every continent, and continues on its way to all the languages which still need a translation of the Bible. This is because the Testament of God is intended for every people and every language.

By the beginning of 1982, the translation of the New Testament in the Ncham language had been checked and tested in its totality with people from many villages. Seven translation consultants went through with a fine tooth-comb and checked the quality of the translation against the original Greek text. Of these consultants, four were from SIL (Katy Barnwell, Ellis Deibler, Ron Stanford, and Mary Steele), and three from UBS (Gilbert Ansre, Jake Loewen and Roger Omanson).

After being checked, the texts were left to be evaluated by the local churches in Bassar for a testing period before publication.

There is a time for everything

During the time when the translation was being read in the churches on Sundays and at meetings during the week, the members of the translation team had a period of rest.

Pastor Gnon Bartholomew Nabine returned to his pastoral ministry in the local Assemblies of God church in Bassar.

Sheila Crunden went home on furlough to Great Britain. She devoted a good part of that time in London to the study of prominence in Ncham discourse. After these studies, Sheila returned to Togo to serve as a translation consultant, to help other translation teams in their work. Two years after undertaking this new role, Sheila returned to England to look after her mother in her old age.

The essential part played by the local church

During this pause in the translation project, a happy event took place in our lives. Honorine and I were united in marriage at the Calvary Temple in Lomé. Honorine had just finished her studies at a Bible college in Nigeria. As a young couple we decided to respond to God's call to serve him full time in His mission. At first, we thought of joining the GBU (University Christian Union), where we had been pioneers in the work with other Christian students on the campus in Lomé : with Granga Daouya, Sadzo Hetsu, Théophile Lawson, Songnaba Arseine, Bazié Souka, Esther Oudrago and many others at the University of Benin (today, the University of Lomé). But Bible translation was the mission to which God in His grace had called us, and that in which we were already involved. So we left for training in linguistics and translation at the CIL course[2] in France, followed by the Field Methods Course in the United Kingdom in the summers of 1982 and 1983, and later at the

---

[2] The *Cours Introductoire en Linguistique* was the French equivalent to the introductory course in linguistics given in English by SIL in anglophone countries.

New Sorbonne University in France. In the academic year 1983-4, we went for theological training at the Irish Baptist College in Belfast.

In 1984, our local church, the Assemblies of God in Lomé II, accepted God's call on our lives, and set us apart for the work of Bible translation as members of Wycliffe in France. As we would then be missionaries from the local church, the church needed to take responsibility for us. Acts 13:1-3 sets out the roles of those working in God's mission: the Holy Spirit sets apart those He has chosen from the local church, and the local church plays its part by commending those who have been chosen to the grace of God for the work, praying for them, and making a contribution to their support. Three things were expected from our local church: to pray regularly for us, and to give monthly for our financial support (which was 25,000 CFA francs, or 500 French francs at that time), and to care for us pastorally during our mission. The missionary vision of our pastor at the time, Pastor Têtêvi Tossou, was a great advantage for us. We had to live by faith from out of these gifts. We knew that we had started out on an uncertain path, at least as far as our financial support was concerned. But the local church took complete responsibility for it. The Lord has shown his faithfulness to us during 32 years of ministry in Bible translation with Wycliffe and SIL. We have never lacked anything. The Good Shepherd of our souls has provided for all our needs, even if sometimes we had periods of want. The Lord has provided for our needs by the participation of the churches involved in our ministry, notably Calvary Temple (Assemblies of God in Togo), and from the Church of Meeting (with Pastor John Leese), as well as from personal friends and family. We could also count on the prayers of our parents who prayed for us every morning at sunrise for many years.

At that time, Wycliffe members were not allowed to speak openly in churches about their financial needs. One simply made a good presentation of the ministry to the partnering churches, whether in Africa or in Europe, and in the same way to personal friends, and allow the Holy Spirit to touch their hearts to commit to supporting us financially. The philosophy behind developing partnerships was that those who were sent, and those who sent and supported them, should all receive personally the call of God and commit to obeying Him voluntarily. This is because God loves all those who give themselves freely and those who give liberally. Jesus assured his disciples in this regard when he said :

> "Truly I tell you, no one who has left home or brothers or sisters or mother or father or children or fields for me and for the gospel will fail to receive a hundred times as much in this present age: homes, brothers, sisters, mothers, children and fields—along with persecutions—and in the age to come eternal life." (Mark 10:29-30)

The Lord watches over his word to accomplish it. I can prove it by the beautiful story of Nenette Jehin, the widow of a Belgian pastor whom God brought along our path. This meeting enabled Madame Jehin to be assured of the call of God on her life to go to the mission field in Africa. She fulfilled this call in Bassar and in Kara with SIL Togo-Benin. Madame Jehin was nicknamed 'Napo's mother' throughout the town of Bassar. She was effectively my adopted mother. When we met Madame Jehin in 1982 in Nîmes in France, we didn't imagine for a moment that it was to reaffirm this word in our lives and in hers.

This approach to developing partnerships has changed in recent years in Wycliffe, but all those who trust in the Lord are never disappointed. The Lord honours those who trust Him, and He shows his generosity to them.

Teaching my people to read

Another member of our Bassar translation team, Samuel Nabine, in collaboration with some young people from the local church (Jonas Poidi, Waké Nikabou, Napo Daré and Tiyadja Faré) gave themselves to promoting literacy. At that time, only a handful of Bassar had learnt to read and write in their own language. The prospect of the imminent publication of the New Testament had stimulated a growing interest in the Christian population to learn to read and write their own language. Also, the testing of the translation with the people in the villages had aroused interest in the stories contained in the Ncham New Testament.

The literacy programme which had begun in 1982 proved a great success ten years later. The scope of this campaign extended as far as neighbouring Ghana, where a large community of Bassar people live. Nine literacy zones were created, each with a supervisor in charge, plus literacy teachers. There were seven zones in Togo and two in Ghana. In Togo, the zones were Bassar, Kabou, Bangéli, Binadjoubé, Dimori, Kalanga, and Tindjassi. In Ghana, there were also literacy zones covering Kpasa and Kpandai in the Volta Region, thanks to the contribution of devoted men such as Manii of Kpasa and Rev. Nambu Emmanuel from Kpandai.

Other results of the translation and literacy programmes

There have been many other results of the translation and literacy programmes in Ncham. Among other things, there was the creation of an arable farm, and also the construction of an artificial lake to provide good drinking water and irrigation for vegetable gardens in the village of Baghan, about 25km south of the town of Bassar.

But the most outstanding of the results of translating the Bible was the birth of a Braille ministry for the blind, who were in effect the 'poorest of the poor'. The Scriptures which had been translated into Ncham would be accessible only to the seeing population. Those who could not see would be left out. They were marginalised in the society. Most of them had become blind as a result of onchocercosis, a disease which affects the retina. In Togo, the region of Baghan is classed as a zone where onchocercosis is rife. It is crossed by a river, the Kama, which is infested by the *onchocera volvulus*, the carrier of this disease which causes blindness. A Centre for the Blind called 'The Bethesda Centre' was built in 1989, thanks to partnership with World Vision International. This project was accomplished thanks to the personal commitment of Paul and Inge Meier of Wycliffe Switzerland.

The Bethesda Centre

The translation of the New Testament was finished in 1982. At that time, we launched a publicity campaign for starting literacy classes in the Bassar region. During this publicity campaign and the opening of literacy classes in that region, the team was confronted by the misery of visually handicapped people. They were destitute and almost forgotten by their relatives, and they were incapable of learning to read and write in Ncham, their mother tongue. They depended on others for all of their needs. What should be done for them? The first thought was to create a project for them as well, so that they could have access to the Holy Scriptures translated into their language. But to do that, it was first necessary to learn the Braille writing system for the blind. But even if that was achieved, the needs of the blind would not be completely provided for. Their need for self-sufficiency within the community still remained.

Although Samuel Nabine and his co-workers were determined to sacrifice themselves to help these destitute people find their place in society, the resources needed for such a project were lacking. Not only did they lack knowledge of braille, but they also lacked the finances for initiating and sustaining such a project. Nevertheless, they decided to submit the problem to the local church, which, to their surprise took it to heart and started to pray to the Lord and to seek the means to help the poverty-stricken blind people.

One day, the team in Bassar received a visit from Paul and Inge Meier. In the course of conversation, the needs of the blind were explained to them. They confessed that for a long time they had felt in their hearts a desire to do something to help the blind in Togo, in the domain of literacy. Paul Meier had already approached certain religious authorities about the needs of the blind population. He was now seeing that this vision for the blind came from God. They needed now to put into action a project for literacy in Braille for the blind. This training project for the blind could be started in the town of Bassar. Together they put their trust in God for the realisation of this vision. The literacy team had already experienced the Lord's provision for their programme. Many literacy classes had started and a good number of those learning to read had made progress in reading and writing their language.

Parallel with the literacy campaign, the team undertook a census of the blind in the whole region. Among about 50,000 inhabitants, they found 500 blind people. The local church, under the leadership of Pastor Gnon Bartholomew and his committee, did not shirk their responsibility. They began to collect gifts from their members to provide for the needs of the blind in the areas affected by onchocercosis.

Generosity encourages generosity

As soon as he returned to Lomé, Paul Meier made an appeal to a Swiss couple, Fritz and Edith Meier, who came to visit Bassar in order to see what was happening in the villages most affected by onchocercosis. After they had visited all the villages, Fritz and Edith were deeply touched by the misery of the blind people. Before leaving, they promised that they would raise support to start the Braille project in Bassar. To bring this promise to fruition, on their return home, this couple sold their house and put part of the sale price towards the project to buy the necessary equipment. Soon afterwards, the project was able to open an office fully equipped for Braille.

A Braille specialist, Richard Steele, who was blind himself learnt of the project and, responded quickly to Paul Meier's appeal. He left America and came to Bassar for two weeks to train a team of teachers in a specialised form of Braille adapted to the Bassar language. Later, Richard became the coordinator with responsibility for external relations between the young Bethesda Centre and their partners. He was assisted in this work by Lois Wilson, a missionary with SIL.

On 11th May 1985, the Bethesda Centre opened officially in a little house with 4 rooms. The course for learning Braille began with a pilot class of six blind students who came from the most affected villages. This pilot class was entirely funded by members of the local church. In spite of their own needs, they regularly sent gifts of food, notably yams, sorghum, maize, sweet potatoes, and also clothes and many other things. From time to time they sent money collected in the parishes. The pastor of the local church and his deacons took turns to come and give messages to the blind students to encourage them. Samuel Nabine, a master tailor by profession, contributed from his own resources to the project. His wife supported their family of seven children with a small business. She became the cook for the pilot class of the Braille students.

Samuel Nabine and his assistant Jonas Poidi, threw themselves body and soul into the work without any salary for about two years. The blind students of the pilot project also needed medical treatment. Happily, SIL Togo-Benin offered to pay for the medicines and other things which were necessary for the well-being of the students.

A new building for the Bethesda Centre

It was during this initial phase that the personnel of the young Bethesda Centre made the acquaintance of World Vision International, through the contacts that I had made with this organisation. On 10th November 1985, World Vision International visited Togo to see the Braille project at close hand.

As a result of this visit, World Vision International agreed to finance the construction of a new building for the Bethesda Centre, and also its running costs for a period of five years. It was expected that at the end of those five years, the Bethesda Centre would have developed its own resources so that its continuation would be assured. World Vision International undertook responsibility for all aspects of the work: literacy in

Braille, construction of the new building, paying the salaries of the staff, the purchase of medicines and food for the students, office equipment, and travel on behalf of the Bethesda Centre. The other partners in the Bethesda Centre, SIL Togo-Benin and CBM (Christoffel Blinden Mission) would also contribute their technical and financial assistance for the running of the Centre, for training and for income generating projects for the support of the Centre. A committee of delegates from the local churches was put in place to supervise the work of the Bethesda Centre. Two members of staff, Jonas Poidi and Napo Daré, received training in mobility for the blind, and in how to manage an arable farm.

The development of agriculture and livestock-breeding for the blind

Until then, the activities of the Bethesda Centre were concentrated on literacy and rehabilitation for the blind. They were all adults, men and women. But the buildings at the Centre were limited, and could not accommodate all the students of both sexes. Only the men were accepted, not the women. This was the first challenge to be faced. The second challenge was the fact that many of these blind people were middle-aged and no longer able to master Braille. So, on arrival at the Bethesda Centre, they had to pass an aptitude test, and those who had fingers which were sensitive to the little pointed dots of the Braille alphabet were able to receive training in literacy for two years. The others were directed towards agriculture, livestock-breeding and mobility training, after which they returned home. There, a member of the Centre staff helped them to set up a little project for raising sheep, goats and chickens, and also a small farm. This approach proved successful, because most of the students had been farmers before being infected with river blindness. The training took about a month, and the students were required to return to the Bethesda Centre every year for at least two to four weeks for a refresher course.

After three years of activity, the Bethesda Centre had trained about twenty blind adults. This number almost tripled five years after the setting up of the Centre. Each student had spent two years under the supervision of the Centre, with follow-up afterwards. Four students of Braille were selected to start a pilot class in French Braille. This initiative naturally opened up wider access to knowledge that had been transcribed into French Braille.

In 1989, the Bethesda Centre started its first pilot farm for agriculture and the raising of sheep. The funding came from the embassy of the United States of America in Togo, which was impressed by the achievements of the Bethesda Centre in Bassar. The farm had the double objective of raising revenue to run the Bethesda Centre, and also to provide animals for the blind which would enable them to start a small stock-breeding project once they had returned home. The farm had an area of six hectares which could be cultivated. Three hectares were used during the first year. The revenue generated by the farm enabled the Bethesda Centre to meet its budget within a few years. As well as those who were students at the Centre, fifty-six other blind people were also helped by this farm. In addition they were all trained in agriculture and in raising sheep and goats. The Centre gave each of them two sheep and some chickens at the end of their training. Some of the blind people were so totally poverty-stricken that a house was built for them in their villages to enable them to integrate into society. The mobility training enabled them to move about alone with the aid of a white stick. The Bethesda Centre even made a football pitch and a volleyball pitch for those who were visually handicapped.

At a short distance from the farm, there is a barrage of water which was made particularly for the people who are victims of river blindness living in the region of Baghan, which is 25km from the town of Bassar. This barrage provides the population with safe drinking water, and also enables them to make vegetable gardens and grow other crops. The barrage has transformed the life of population. Thanks to the partnership with JAARS,[3] a team led by Mike Reece made two visits to the area to bring this project to completion.

The Bethesda Blind Centre was open to those of any religion without discrimination. There were regular times of Bible study and prayer organised for the blind students, but these were not obligatory. The relaxed atmosphere at every meeting enabled all the students to participate. During the first five years of the existence of the Centre, only one blind student declined the appeal to accept Jesus Christ as Saviour and Lord. All those who passed through the Bethesda Centre received Jesus and were baptised. They all went home as true witnesses for Christ in their respective villages.

The translation of the Bible is central to the development of a people

The translation of the Bible is central to the development of an ethnic and linguistic group. The reason is simple. The translation is the base on which the three pillars of life for

---

[3] JAARS Inc. is a nonprofit organisation which helps the Wycliffe Global Alliance, SIL International, and other organizations get practical, day-to-day support for Bible translation. JAARS focuses on five areas: aviation, land transportation, water transportation, information technology, and media.

all peoples rest: that is, the spiritual, the intellectual, and the physical.

The first pillar is of a spiritual nature, the pillar of religion. It is on this pillar that the spiritual, moral and psychological life of a people rests. It is the foundation for the values which govern the world-view of the people in question: its relation with itself, with others, with the rest of society, and with the whole universe. It is the foundation for knowing how to live: with oneself, with others, with the universe, and with God. In other words, it is the pillar of wisdom based either on ancestral beliefs or on the truths of the Bible.

The second pillar is intellectual in nature, that of reason. On this pillar rests the intelligence which permits a person to understand him or herself, to understand others, society, the environment, and the universe. Intelligence gives human beings the knowledge of how to perform tasks, and this knowledge is the source of science and technology, which permit us to master all the skills necessary for human life.

The third pillar is that of human resources. It refers to the physical stamina necessary for defence against attack from outside, but also necessary to promote stability within an ethnic and linguistic group. This requires training, using written language to transfer knowledge and competence in various fields. The Bible, in the book of Daniel, teaches us that even God has such a defence. The Archangel Michael is called the General of the Lord's Armies. In the book of Numbers, the stories of Balaam and of Joshua tell us much about it. Jesus says in the Gospel that his Father has legions of angels ready for combat. When he was arrested in the Garden of Gethsemane, he said to Peter: "Do you think that I cannot call on my Father, and he will at once put at my disposal more than twelve legions of angels ? But how then would the Scriptures be fulfilled that it must happen this way ?" (Matthew 26 :53-4).

The Greeks and the Romans often talked about 'a healthy mind in a healthy body'. The maintenance of a healthy body for its own security and that of the community necessitates an education involving the use of language. The maintenance of order and the defence of the walls of the city rest on this pillar.

The ruin of a civilisation is progressive. It begins with the moral and spiritual protecting walls, and continues with the intellectual walls and ends with the deterioration of human relations symbolised by troubles in society and destructive behaviour. All the ancient civilisations crumbled in this way.

In the same way, the development, or the restoration, of the peoples of Africa follows the same pattern. It begins with spiritual and moral revival within ethnolinguistic groups, continues by scientific and technological innovations, and finishes with the re-establishment of stability within and defence against enemy forces without.

The case of the restoration of the people of Israel in the time of Nehemiah is a concrete example. First of all, the necessary information was brought to Nehemiah. This produced in him an awakened conscience. He found out how bad the ruin of Jerusalem was, and the shame in which his people found themselves.

The action which Nehemiah took was first of all to re-establish the relationship between the people and their God. For this to happen, he first needed to restore, or rather to heal, the relationships among the people themselves. For Nehemiah, to ill-treat your brother was to sin against God

The centrality of Bible translation

(Nehemiah 5). He decided first to set up the pillar of reconciliation, which means not only a spiritual relationship with God but also with your fellow human beings. To encourage this atmosphere he turned to Ezra to teach Biblical values; not in a foreign language, but in everyday Hebrew. The Exile far from the Holy Land had resulted in the language of the Bible being forgotten. It was this which gave birth to the ministry of translating the Bible.

Secondly, Nehemiah turned to men who were skilled and capable and who knew how to restore normality to civil society. This is the pillar of the intellect. Finally, he organised defence against interior and exterior enemies. The builders also became fighters and spies. He organised the police, a physical force to protect them.

The story of the creation of man reveals that the first thing which God did after having made human beings was to speak His word to them. He spoke to Adam and Eve, and told them that the creation was there for them to enjoy, to cultivate and take pleasure in. "God blessed them and said to them, 'Be fruitful and increase in number; fill the earth and subdue it. Rule over the fish in the sea and the birds in the sky and over every living creature that moves on the ground." (Genesis 1:28).

The translation of the Word of God, the Bible, into local languages brings first of all a basis for the spiritual, moral and artistic education of the people. Secondly, it gives a foundation for intellectual and technological education—all the knowledge and techniques which enable people to understand, master, organise and exploit their environment and the resources which are necessary for their lives.

Because of this, the ministry of Bible translation is not simply a question of the translation of 'the Book' into a language, but goes much further. The language of a people is the foundation upon which all the pillars of their life are built. The mother tongue is a means for transmitting all the wisdom which guides our way of life from one generation to another. As Nelson Mandela aptly said, "when you speak to someone in a language he understands, it goes into his head. When you speak to him in his mother tongue, it goes into his heart."

The translation of the Bible is a means of solving the problems of our world, a world which is in crisis from top to bottom. The Bible lays the proper foundation for a rediscovery of the great universal values which are for every community of human beings on this earth: truth, justice, respect, liberty, love, forgiveness, and peace. The Word of God translated into a community's language opens God's way for it to escape from the spirals of greed, excess, and the fear of the future. Through the conversion of each person, the Word leads human beings into wisdom, which results in liberty and a sense of responsibility, according to the words of Jesus, the Son of God: "If the Son makes you free, you will be free indeed." (John 8 :36).

Chapter 3

The Bible translation movement in Togo

The route that we took as a couple led us into full-time service in the mission of Bible translation. In the summer of 1984, we were accepted as members of Wycliffe France for Bible translation. From there, we returned to Togo as members of SIL International, assigned to the Togo-Benin Branch, to finish the project of translating the New Testament into the Bassar language. But at the same time, we were burning with the desire to share the vision for Bible translation with the churches in Togo. We consecrated the whole of 1985 to achieve these two objectives.

Our strategy for sharing this vision was to establish personal contacts with church leaders, to create trust, and to develop relations with the local churches that they led. We succeeded in gaining letters of authorisation from the Rev. Eli Kofi Ayivi, Moderator of the Evangelical Presbyterian Church of Togo, and from Rev. Djakouté Mitré, President of the Assemblies of God, to visit all the parishes of the two major protestant denominations in Togo at the time.

Text of the letter of authorisation to speak in the churches of the Evangelical Church of Togo, dated 7th December 1984

> Dear Brethren and Colleagues,
>
> The Protestant Churches in Togo have always had the deep desire that everyone should be able to read and understand the Bible in their mother tongue. The Summer Institute of Linguistics, an organisation recognised by the government of Togo, has as its aim the translation of the Word of God into vernacular languages. Because of this, we want to take the opportunity of recommending Napo POIDI, an active member of this Society, and to authorise him to speak in our meetings to explain the importance and necessity of translating the Bible into Bassar and other languages.
>
> I want to thank you for your confidence in us, and for your collaboration in the advancement of the Lord's work. This letter comes with fraternal greetings in Christ.
>
> Yours sincerely in Him,
>
> Pastor Eli Kofi Ayivi
>
> President of the Christian Council of Togo

The visits to the churches began in Lomé and continued into the interior of the country, going from town to town according to a pre-planned itinerary and covering the whole country. Every Sunday we were in a parish to speak about the necessity of translating the Bible into our languages. Thanks to the talent of Liberty Aziadekey, a teacher who was a friend from university days, as interpreter, our message was translated from French into Ewe for the churches in the south of the country. In the north of the country, each parish chose its own interpreter. It was like this as far as Dapaong, the northernmost large town in Togo.

This first tour of the churches to make known the work of translating the Bible into the local languages aimed to raise awareness in the Body of Christ in Togo for this vital ministry in the Church. The positive effect was immediately felt by the SIL teams working in the translation projects which were already in progress at the time. But most satisfying was the positive reaction of the Togolese churches towards the translation of the Bible into our languages.

The completion of the Bassar New Testament

In 1986, a preliminary edition of the New Testament in Bassar was produced. What remained to be done was to reconstitute the translation team with its original members, Samuel Nabine, Pastor Gnon and myself, and revise the preliminary edition which had been submitted for reading within the churches. Then this edition had to be systematically revised by groups of reviewers from the three Christian denominations in Bassar, separately from the work of the translation team.

In November 1988, and in February and May 1989, the quality of this revised preliminary edition was checked again by two SIL translation consultants: the Epistle to the Romans by Ron Stanford, and the rest of the New Testament books by Mary Steele, who worked in collaboration with the translation team and reviewers delegated by the local churches of the

Assemblies of God, the Baptists and the Catholics. Mary Steele spent a month with the team for the final translation check. This last stage brought to completion the process of translating the New Testament into the Bassar Ncham language.

After that came the next phase in the process of publishing this translation of the New Testament in Ncham. It began with the typesetting of the translation. This would take at least three months. It was begun on 5th February 1990, and ended in May of the same year, at the Centre of Wycliffe UK at Horsleys Green in the United Kingdom. David Crozier, a computer specialist, and myself worked without interruption for three months to prepare the text of the New Testament for printing in South Korea. However, one might ask why the typesetting took such a long time?

At that time, translators produced draft translations of the biblical texts, written by hand. At least, that was so for us. These manuscripts were then typed on a typewriter. All the corrections which were made as the text was being read meant that the whole text had to be typed again. The work was slow, and demanded careful attention by the translators. This was before the first computers were used in Bible translation projects. There were none of the useful, productive computer programmes that we have today, such as Paratext. So we had to check manually that all the verses of the New Testament had been translated, and that key terms such as 'grace', 'faith', 'love', 'hope', had all been spelt in the same way throughout the New Testament. Other important aspects of the work consisted of checking that all the mistakes had been corrected, and that the punctuation, harmonisation of vocabulary, key biblical terms, Biblical names, illustrations of unknown objects, explanatory footnotes, glossary and maps, all conformed to the standard required. All this had to be done by the vigilance of the technician and the translator, reading and re-reading the text as many times as necessary. This took much time. Happily, since then there has been progress in information technology. New programmes have been created and improved to facilitate the production and composition of translated texts of high quality.

Translating the Bible into a language is without doubt one of the most difficult tasks in life. In our African context, it can be compared with bringing up children. The most difficult task is to help the child to find meaning in his life. Both tasks need first of all God's help, and after that the contribution of many others, because it cannot be done on one's own. Thanks to the contribution of another partner, the financial resources were provided to print 2000 copies of the final edition of the Bassar New Testament. This partner was the International Bible Society (IBS), who agreed to finance the publication. But we had to wait a year while the funds were raised until the first copies came from the printers. For the hundreds of men and women who were speakers of Ncham and who had been learning for several years how to read and write their language, it was a moment which had been eagerly awaited. For the translation team itself, the joy was indeed great. But they were indebted to those who had shared with them in the Bassar translation project, a big family of personal friends and all the partners in the project: SIL, the Bible Society (UBS), and all the unknown people who had supported the translation with their encouragement and their prayers. Thanks to the collaboration of all of them, this New Testament saw the light of day. Each of those who had played their part can therefore confidently expect their reward, promised by God, on the day when our Lord and Saviour Jesus Christ returns. Because they have sown in tears before God, they will reap with joy.

We reap what we sow

If it is true that we reap what we sow, then an analysis of this fascinating story of the Bassar New Testament leads us to the sad conclusion that an in-depth contribution from the local church toward the realisation of the New Testament translation project was lacking.

Let us consider a Biblical example. Let us see what King David did, the man who received from God himself the testimony that he was a man after God's own heart. To atone for his sin of having ordered a census of his people (which was the prerogative of God who alone had control of the life of his people Israel in his hands), and to appease the wrath of God which had fallen on the people, he refused Araunah's offer of the sacrifice which he had to make to the Lord:

> But the king replied to Araunah, 'No, I insist on paying you for it. I will not sacrifice to the LORD my God burnt offerings that cost me nothing.' So David bought the threshing-floor and the oxen and paid 50 shekels of silver for them. David built an altar to the LORD there and sacrificed burnt offerings and fellowship offerings. (II Samuel 24:24-25a)

Even though he had the opportunity to acquire freely the land and the cattle for his sacrifice to God without making any effort on his part, David preferred to invest, to sow for God a seed which cost him something and which had value before God. Rather than relying on human beings, he wanted to show that everything he was and had belonged to God in whom he trusted to receive mercy. This is what he said to the prophet Gad:

David said to Gad, 'I am in deep distress. Let us fall into the hands of the LORD, for his mercy is great ; but do not let us fall into human hands.' (II Samuel 24:14)

The history of the modern world teaches us that even though France's hero, General de Gaule, was grateful for what the allies, the Americans, the British, the Canadians and the Russians, had done for the liberation of France, he was indignant that the French Resistance had not been implicated in or associated with the landing of the allies in Normandy on D-Day, 6th June 1944.

We believe that the involvement of the local church is essential for the progress of mission, and in particular for the translation of the Bible into the mother tongue, for the salvation of the Bibleless peoples in Africa. God answers prayer and He sees the good works of his people in every place where they are found, and He rejoices when his people share in His work, in answer to his call.

An analysis of the context in which God raised up the mission of Wycliffe in the 14th century shows that this context is closely linked to the life and activities of the local church. In the 14th century, the local church prayed to God, sought his face, even heard him speak by prophecy, words of wisdom and of knowledge, but it no longer trembled before the authority of the Testament which God left for the Church, the Bible. The local church had abandoned its loyalty to the Holy Scriptures. The provision of Biblical truth and an appetite for the Word of God was rare within it. Reading and meditation on the Bible had no place in the church services. In its place there was only drama, exhortations and enticing stories in the Church. This confirms what the Holy Spirit says in 1 Timothy 4:1-2:

"The Spirit clearly says that in later times some will abandon the faith and follow deceiving spirits and things taught by demons. Such teachings come through hypocritical liars, whose consiences are seared as with a hot iron." The Apostle Paul in the same chapter shows the way to a solution for the young leader Timothy in these terms: "Until I come, devote yourself to the public reading of Scripture, to preaching and to teaching. Do not neglect your gift, which was given to you through prophecy when the body of elders laid their hands on you." (I Timothy 4 :13-14). In this way, the young pastor Timothy had to apply himself to reading the Holy Scriptures and exhorting the Christians to do the same. But how would he do that if he disregarded them, or if he had no access to them at all in a language that he understood ?

Following the same line of thought, John Wycliffe said (and I quote him): "To ignore the Scripture is to ignore Christ." John Wycliffe was at the time a professor in the prestigious University of Oxford, and he insisted on the supreme authority of the Bible in his teaching. For taking this position he was dismissed from his post. In this way, the sole revelation of God, sure and infallible, the Word of God inspired by the Holy Spirit, had lost its place in the local church of the 14th century. Confronting this situation in the church, God raised up 'the mission of Wycliffe'. The work of John Wycliffe and his collaborators would serve as a precursor of the Reformation movement in the Church two centuries later. This action consisted of translating the Bible into English and teaching it to ordinary people in order to correct errors. They translated it into the common language to make it accessible so that it would speak for itself to ordinary people. They themselves lived simple and sacrificial lives. They preached love and the forgiveness of sins freely through the perfect work of our Lord Jesus Christ. For John Wycliffe and his co-workers "All Scripture is God-breathed and is useful for teaching, rebuking, correcting and training in righteousness." (II Timothy 3 :16). From this came the famous expression: "John Wycliffe, the Morning Star of the Reformation in the Church". This movement took shape in the local church and impacted the community outside of the church. In the course of time, the Bible found its place again in the life of the Church in England and in Scotland, where it was read and studied avidly in all the homes in the country.[1]

This experience is certainly not unique in the history of the Christian Church. But what does the Church need most to fulfil her mission today? Good preaching? More miracles in the Church? More proclamation of the Gospel? Or more manifestations of the Holy Spirit? The tension is palpable in the Body of Christ, but it provides a unique opportunity to change the model and work together towards a common goal if we want to engage afresh in spiritual revival.

Wycliffe's mission was not limited to the translation of the Bible into his own language, English. It went beyond that by involving the local church through the witness of the 'Lollards', the 'preaching evangelists', also called 'the disciples of Wycliffe'. Their witness called people not only to repentance from sin, which had led Christ to the cross of Calvary for the salvation of all who believe, but also they proclaimed the supremacy of the message of the whole Bible. The message that 'the just shall live by faith' comes from the Holy Scriptures. It was into the darkness of people's sin that God sent the light of his Word translated into contemporary English in order to transform their lives.

If the local church is not involved in the realisation and the diffusion of the translation of the Bible into its own languages,

---

[1]Bridge, Donald, *Power Evangelism and the Word of God*, Kingsway Publications Ltd, 1987.

she abrogates her responsibility to look for solutions to resolve her own problems. The contribution from external partners alone is an advantage but at the same time a handicap for the Continent. This is because, rightly or wrongly, it shows that Africa is incapable of making decisions regarding her development on her own. We are sounding the alarm about this, and are calling for a greater sense of responsibility towards the translation and diffusion of the Bible in local languages. Local African churches should affirm loud and long the supreme authority of the message of the Bible over all other teachings given in the churches throughout the Continent. The way to reach that goal is to promote a quality translation of the Biblical message, together with the need for learning to read it, so that the Scriptures in the mother tongues of Africa will be used by everybody: pastors, theologians, evangelists and other movers and shakers in the Church.

But there are other big obstacles in the way. When the various resolutions about Bible translation are made at consultations and conferences, it is very rare that any take into consideration the need to engage the local African church in the Bible translation movement across Africa. Africa is not associated with the work, nor is her help solicited, and unfortunately she doesn't complain about it! Even if she is involved, it is in a superficial capacity which doesn't go to the heart of the problem. The culture of dependency on outside resources takes precedence over the development of partnerships within Africa. This has unexpected consequences. For example, one day a church leader made the following surprising remark to us: "Why does Wycliffe-Togo want our church to take responsibility for the support of our missionary when its overseas partner says it will underwrite this support? In that case, we will preserve our meagre resources!"

Furthermore, the Apostle Paul, in his letter to the Philippians, says the following about giving to missionaries: "Not that I desire your gifts; what I desire is that more be credited to your account." (Philippians 4:17). In other words, when the local Church gives her resources for a good cause like the translation of the Bible into her language, she increases God's blessing on her account. This is because, as the Apostle Paul says in pursuing his argument: "They are a fragrant offering, an acceptable sacrifice, pleasing to God. And my God will meet all your needs according to the riches of his glory in Christ Jesus." (Philippians 4:18c-19)

All this shows that the involvement of the local African churches in financing the translation and diffusion of the Bible in their mother tongues should be constantly promoted in the churches in Africa. Local, national and regional strategies need to be adopted. The well-being of Africa depends on it, according to this word of the Lord Jesus Christ: "It is more blessed to give than to receive." (Acts 20:35)

Now, do we believe that this feeling of helplessness proclaimed by the local African church comes from the poverty others have always recognised in Africa? Africa is in fact the richest continent in the world! Instead of being worried, we should unload this burden on to the Lord, as well as all the other burdens which obstruct our effective engagement in the mission of translating the Bible in Africa. For the Lord God has said, "I am who I am". Because the one who is called "I am" is with us, we shall certainly succeed.

The Gospels recount that one day, in front of a crowd of five thousand hungry people, Jesus said to his disciples: "You give them something to eat." The reply the disciples gave shows that the sacrifice necessary for feeding such a large crowd was impossible for them.

> They said to him, 'That would take more than half a year's wages! Are we to go and spend that much on bread and give it to them to eat?' 'How many loaves do you have ?' he asked. 'Go and see.' When they found out, they said, 'Five – and two fish.' (Mark 6:37-38)

Thereupon the disciples gave to Jesus the little they had to feed the crowd.

In response to a question from a Togolese journalist about the position traditional chiefs hold in African society, one chief, as the guarantor of the traditions of his people, said this: "We, the traditional chiefs, are there for our people and our people are there for us." This simple reply tells us much about African thinking, which is "I am because we are", contrary to Western thought, which is "I think, therefore I am". African thinking always gives priority to human relationships, that is the legendary solidarity which has shaped Africa and which is also found at the heart of the message of the Apostle Paul to the Corinthians: "Just as the body, though one, has many parts, but all its parts form one body, so it is with Christ." (I Corinthians 12:12)

Let us take advantage of this legendary African solidarity and work together to remove whatever hinders the establishment of a lasting movement for the translation and diffusion of the Bible in our African languages. This would at least enable the whole of Africa to follow in the steps of the poor widow who put into the temple treasury all that she had to live on, because of her love for God:

> Jesus sat down opposite the place where the offerings were put and watched the crowd putting

their money into the temple treasury. Many rich people threw in large amounts. But a poor widow came and put in two very small copper coins, worth only a few pence. Calling his disciples to him, Jesus said, 'Truly I tell you, this poor widow has put more into the treasury than all the others. They all gave out of their wealth ; but she, out of her poverty, put in everything – all she had to live on.' (Mark 12:41-44)

The local African church should not make her poverty an excuse, because the Bible clearly says the following in the book of Proverbs 22:7: "The rich rule over the poor, and the borrower is slave to the lender." Africa must now free herself from this label which people attach to her and behave like the poor widow in front of Jesus Christ in the Temple.

The local African church has a duty before God to take her responsibility seriously and to participate effectively in the mission of translating and propagating the Bible, and in all other mission activities among African peoples. To my mind, this is the way that she will be able to affirm with conviction the supreme authority of biblical values over against the secular drift which is currently influencing African societies. This is substantially what is written in the book of Proverbs chapter 22 cited above, in verse 6: "Start children off on the way they should go, and even when they are old they will not turn from it." The role of the Wycliffe mission in Africa is to give to the young African church the necessary information to equip her to participate effectively in the Mission of God in Africa through the translation of the Bible for her own peoples.

The total engagement of the local African Church will be a long process, and will require setting up strategies to enable her to come out of the mindset of dependency to which she has been subjugated for more than a century. These strategies must also see the leadership of the local churches involved in the structures supporting the Bible translation movement. Committee members from local Churches should be at the core of every organisation involved in the Bible translation movement, so that every translation project will be at the centre of the ministry of the local church concerned, and also of the ethnic and linguistic community which will benefit.

But in most cases, the reality on the ground is completely different. Church committees are sidelined within the structures of local and national Bible translation organisations, either through ignorance or deliberately. In the end, the local church seems anonymous, isolated from the decisions of national translation organisations. Little by little these organisations have become independent of the authority of the local church which they are supposed to represent. Worse still, these structures dominate the Bible translation movement, and so inhibit the positive effects brought about by Bible translation on the local church and the language communities among which that church is called to live by faith.

The lack of effective engagement by the local church and community—and the absence of their participation in the decisions taken by the leaders of the Bible translation movement—automatically engender a lack of financial, material and spiritual participation of that church in the work of Bible translation. Worse still, it delays the local church's engagement in using the translations in the local languages. Rather, as we shall see in the following case, it is the duty of the local church to emphasise the spiritual value of translating the Bible into a local language throughout the organisation.

In reality, the translation of the Bible has a three-fold value: first of all, the Bible in the local language continually reminds the local Church of their vocation to be salt and light in the world, according to these words in II Peter 1:13: "I think it is right to refresh your memory as long as I live in the tent of this body". Secondly, the value of a Bible translation consists in the transformation of the receptor communities by the continuous propagation of the Holy Scriptures in the local languages, from one generation to the next. Finally, the translation of the Bible gives the local church the means of developing a liturgy which is purely biblical, that is to say the Word of God clothed in prayer in the heart language of the people of God. "Through Jesus, therefore, let us continually offer to God a sacrifice of praise – the fruit of lips that openly profess his name." (Hebrews 13:15).

An important occasion : the dedication of 'God's Book'

The language spoken by the Bassar people is called 'Bassar'. It is also called 'Ncham'. The name 'Ncham' (which is spelt in the Bassar orthography 'ncam') is derived from the root '-ca', which means 'smith', because the Bassar in Togo were known for their expertise in the extracting and smelting of iron ore.[2] The Ncham or Bassar language is spoken by about 200,000 people found in Togo (which is French-speaking) and in Ghana (which is English-speaking).

The Ncham language has two dialects: 'Mpeetim' and 'Nfum' or 'Ntaapum'. The principal difference between the two dialects is that the first, 'Mpeetim', uses the particle 'pee' more often, where the second, 'Nfum', uses 'fu'. In Togo, the first,

---

[2]Candice Goucher (1985). "The Iron Industry of Bassar, Togo : An Interdisciplinary Investigation of African Technological History". PhD thesis. Los Angeles: University of California Los Angeles.

'Mpeetim', is spoken in the principal town of the Prefecture of Bassar and the surrounding area, and also in the second largest town, Kabou. Because of this, the dialect 'Mpeetim' is the most widespread and thus the most studied. In Ghana, the two communities live together in the locations where the Bassar community is found. In their research comparing the two dialects, Mary Abbott and Monica Cox observed that the Mpeetim dialect which they had studied in Ghana was the same as the one they found when they came to Bassar in Togo in 1967. It was the 'prestige' dialect, that is to say it was the one most widely understood by all the Bassar speakers.

The decision concerning the 'prestige' dialect is of the utmost importance before beginning a translation of the Bible in any language. The choice of the Mpeetim dialect for translating the New Testament and the Old Testament into Ncham was very wise. The principal variations between the two dialects are first of all regular: the noun classes and their derivative suffixes which are '-ti' or '-di' in Mpeetim are pronounced '–ri', '-ni' or '-li' in Nfum. For example: in Mpeetim, 'ubɔti' *chief*, 'bìiti' *uncover*, 'bɔ̀nti' *darken*, 'dibindi' *chest (anatomical)*, are pronounced 'ubɔri', 'bìiri', 'bɔnnì', 'libinli' in Nfum.

The verbal suffixes with the form '-fi' in Mpeetim are pronounced '-hi' in Nfum. For example: 'bifí' *learn,* and 'pilfí' *listen,* are pronounced 'bihì' and 'pilhì' in Nfum.

The affixes of the noun class di/a in Mpeetim become li/ŋ in Nfum. For example: 'diyil'/ 'ayil' *head/heads* are pronounced 'liyil' and 'ŋyil' in Nfum.

Then there are some irregular forms: in Mpeetim, four auxiliary verbs bíi, pée, du, kpáàa are pronounced 'bí', 'fúù', 'di', 'kpàa' in Nfum, while the prominence particle 'dí' in Mpeetim is pronounced 'ní' in Nfum.

Another difficulty to be overcome in creating an orthography for the Bassar language is that of marking the tone. In a tonal language, a difference in the pitch of the voice, which is called the 'tone', can alter the meaning of a word which would otherwise have the same consonants and vowels. Accents are often used to mark the tonal differences of words in the orthography of a tonal language. The fact that English orthography does not use accents, and that French uses them for a different purpose, is an additional difficulty for the speakers of Bassar in English-speaking Ghana who are used to an orthography without accents. The fact that French uses accents to mark vowel quality and not tone is a similar difficulty for French-speaking Togolese.

Even though these few variations are recognised between the two dialects, and between the speakers on both sides of the Togo-Ghana border, the differences do not present an obstacle to mutual comprehension, as we have seen. Moreover, nobody denies the feeling of belonging to one and the same people-group, speaking the same language. The translation of the Bible can be made with the assurance that it will be accepted by all Bassar speakers.

As far as religion is concerned, the Bassar people practise the traditional religion of their ancestors. The first evangelists to tread on Bassar soil were Catholic missionaries in the 1930s. The very first missionary was Father Emmanuel Kennis, of the Society of African Missions (SMA), who arrived in 1933. Later, Pentecostal missionaries of the American Mission of the Assemblies of God came, led by Pastor Wakefield, who arrived in 1951. Even though these churches have been planted in nearly every Bassar village, the number of Bassar Christians is still less than 10% of the Ncham-speaking population.

On 4th January 1992, an historic event took place in the life of the Bassar people: the dedication of the New Testament in the Ncham language. On the one hand, the event set out to dedicate to God a work that was accomplished by His grace, and which translated His love into the tongue of the Bassar people; on the other, it was a presentation of this wonderful spiritual tool which can make people wise for salvation by faith in Jesus Christ. It was for the Bassar people in general, and to the Body of Christ in particular, who are called to dispense the grace of the Lord among the Bassar people. Considered from this angle, the event on 4th January was a real visitation of God to the people.

Because of this, the dedication undoubtedly had a two-fold significance. The first was spiritual, and marked the opening by God of direct access for the Bassar people to His salvation and to the Kingdom of His well-beloved Son Jesus Christ. Remember that they had had to wait for thirty years from the time that the first two linguist-translators from SIL had begun their research on the Ncham language! The translation had been accomplished with the cooperation of a number of native Bassar translators, seven translation consultants from SIL and the Bible Society (UBS), not forgetting the moral, spiritual and especially financial support of many friends from Switzerland, the UK, the USA and others.

The second significance was cultural, and laid both Scriptural and literary foundations by giving the Ncham language an appropriate writing system. With this fundamental work, God opened a royal and sure way for the people. They could now pass from the traditional oral civilisation to a new civilisation based on the written language, and be able to face effectively the challenges of the modern age.

The dedication of a New Testament in a language is really a holy convocation before the Lord and Saviour of all people. The participation of the maximum number of people in the celebration is essential. The team responsible for the organisation of this ceremony expected the involvement of all the Bassar people, and particularly those who were already members of the Body of Christ. It was more than simply a celebration of 'God's Book' in the Ncham language; it was really the entry into the town of Bassar of Jesus Christ, the Son of God, translated into the Bassar language. For this the four Christian denominations among the Bassar people–Assemblies of God, Catholic, Presbyterian and Baptist–formed a committee which dealt with everything to do with the practical and spiritual organisation of this celebration.

Among the first people to be invited were the political and administrative leaders of the Prefecture of Bassar: the Chief Administrative Officer or Prefect, the Mayor of the town of Bassar, a representative of the Togolese government and the Paramount Chief of the Bassar people. After them, each canton and village in Bassar was represented by two delegations. One delegation was led by the chief of the Canton and the village, the traditional leaders with their retinues, who represented the local people. Then there was a delegation of the Christian community of the canton or the village. Delegations from the four corners of Togo and from overseas were also present. Most important of these were the national representatives of the four main Christian denominations in Togo. Also present was a delegation from the Bassar diaspora in Ghana, and representatives of SIL and the Bible Society. Added to these was the population of Bassar and the surrounding countryside. Despite the troubled times, both socially and politically, and also the cool and dusty weather of the harmattan season, the attendance that Saturday, 4th January 1992–market day in the town of Bassar–was huge and spontaneous.

The dedication of the Bassar New Testament, the first to be translated in Togo since its independence in 1960, was in fact a prophetic event, in the sense that it did not come about by the will of man who had planned and achieved it, but by the will of God.

Convinced of the certainty of the truth of Holy Scripture, the workers in the Bassar translation project had taken to heart the mission of interceding on behalf of the people, as it is written: "See, today I appoint you over nations and kingdoms to uproot and tear down, to destroy and overthrow, to build and to plant." (Jeremiah 1 :10). So the whole Christian community identified with the people and interceded for several months for the mercy and forgiveness of God for all the people. On 4th January 1992 the Bible texts for that day, Deuteronomy 33 :26-29, were used as the basis for intercession :

> Moses also said:
>
> "There is no one like the God of Jeshurun,
> who rides across the heavens to help you
> and on the clouds in his majesty.
> The eternal God is your refuge,
> and underneath are the everlasting arms.
> He will drive out your enemies before you,
> saying, 'Destroy them!'
>
> So Israel will live in safety;
> Jacob will dwell secure
> in a land of grain and new wine,
> where the heavens drop dew.
>
> Blessed are you, Israel!
> Who is like you,
> a people saved by the LORD ?
> He is your shield and helper

and your glorious sword.
Your enemies will cower before you, and you will tread on their heights."

The second text was taken from the book of Ezekiel 34:23-31:

> I will place over them one shepherd, my servant David, and he will tend them; he will tend them and be their shepherd. I the LORD will be their God, and my servant David will be prince among them. I the LORD have spoken. I will make a covenant of peace with them and rid the land of savage beasts so that they may live in the wilderness and sleep in forests in safety, I will make them and the places surrounding my hill a blessing. I will send down showers in season; there will be showers of blessing. The trees will yield their fruit and the ground will yield its crops; the people will be secure in their land. They will know that I am the LORD, when I break the bars of their yoke and rescue them from the hands of those who enslaved them. They will no longer be plundered by the nations, nor will wild animals devour them. They will live in safety, and no one will make them afraid. I will provide for them a land renowned for its crops, and they will no longer be victims of famine in the land or bear the scorn of the nations. Then they will know that I, the LORD their God, am with them and that they, the Israelites, are my people, declares the Sovereign LORD. You are my sheep, the sheep of my pasture, and I am your God, declares the Sovereign LORD."

Finally, the third text was from I Corinthians 15:57: 'But thanks be to God! He gives us the victory through our Lord Jesus Christ.'

Today we can be certain that a true covenant in Jesus Christ has been established between God and the Bassar people, and we see it in the members of the Body of Christ called out from among the Bassar people. In the book of the Acts of the Apostles we read the following:

> Simon has described to us how God first intervened to choose a people for his name from the Gentiles. The words of the prophets are in agreement with this, as it is written:
>
>> "After this I will return and rebuild David's fallen tent. Its ruins I will rebuild, and I will restore it, that the rest of mankind may seek the Lord, even all the Gentiles who bear my name, says the Lord who does these things - things known from long ago."
>
> (Acts 15:14-18)

The prophetic import of the launch of the Bassar New Testament is the beginning of the conquest of the peoples of all the languages spoken in Togo and beyond, through translating the Bible. This is to fulfil the word of the Psalmist: "Ask me, and I will make the nations your inheritance, the ends of the earth your possession." (Psalm 2:8)

The impact of the celebration

The salient points of the programme for that day, 4th January 1992, were of three kinds: the speeches, the prayer of dedication, and also the speeches made by the translators of the New Testament. For the first time also, a speech was translated and read in the Bassar language to the thousands of people assembled for the ceremony in the large municipal football stadium in the town of Bassar.

Four speeches were made, one after another. It was my privilege to make the first, on behalf of the Christian community of Bassar. I expressed the gratitude of all Bassar Christians to God, and then petitioned Him on behalf of the the people. Then followed the speech of Eric Bartels, the director of SIL in Togo and Benin. After presenting the work of SIL throughout the world, Mr. Bartels concluded by saying that the New Testament translated into the Ncham language was the gift of God to the people in their mother tongue. The third speech was made by the Paramount Chief of Bassar, on behalf of all the traditional chiefs of the people. He rejoiced in the salvation brought to his people through Jesus Christ, the Son of God. The final speech was made by the Chief Government Officer (Prefet) of Bassar. He presented the Prefecture of Bassar as one of the largest in the country. He made a list of all the riches hidden under the soil of the Prefecture, and then he thanked Almighty God for his grace towards all the people of Bassar. All the speakers thanked the many partners and friends who had supported the translation project by their gifts and their prayers over three decades. They desired that the Word of God should find its place in the heart of the Bassar people for their development.

Finally, the translators were given the opportunity to speak. They described briefly how the translation project began in 1962 when a team settled in Lungi in Ghana, how they started to study the Ncham language, and then the process of translation. The translators thanked their friends and their partner churches, as well as the Bassar people in Togo and in Ghana who had been with them during the nearly 30 years that the project had taken. The celebration was punctuated by songs of praise to God and ended with a reception given at the Catholic Mission of Bassar.

Portions of the celebration of the New Testament in Ncham were broadcast by the national media. In fact, the showing of the film of the dedication of the Ncham New Testament on national television aroused a keen interest among Christians of other ethnic groups in the country. We received messages of congratulation from many places, and particularly appeals that translation work should be done in other local languages of the country. In response to these many appeals, we decided to organise a first meeting bringing together key people belonging to twelve ethnic and linguistic groups who were interested in the translation of the Bible into their mother tongues. A total of 36 people responded to our invitation, three representatives from each ethnic and linguistic group. This historic meeting took place over a meal on Thursday, 2nd April 1992 at the Hôtel du Golf in Lome. This event marked the beginning of the story of the Association Wycliffe Togo for the Translation of the Bible and for Literacy (AWT). We will speak of the birth of this association later.

The translation of the Old Testament into Ncham (Bassar)

The project to translate the Old Testament into Ncham was the next logical step after the success of the translation of the New Testament. The day after the dedication, an association of Bassar churches, ACEB (Association of Bassar Christian Churches), was born out of the committee of churches which had been formed for the organisation of the dedication of the New Testament.

From 1992, ACEB, led by its secretary at the time, Nadjombe Makou, and by its treasurer Father Davis Mekkattuparambil, contacted SIL Togo-Benin, which had helped in the translation of the New Testament, with a view to translating the Old Testament. This first contact did not achieve its purpose, so ACEB was directed to the Bible Society of Togo, but this organisation wanted to work with the association under a partnership arrangement. This would mean that the costs of the translation work (salaries and equipment) would be divided equally between the Bible Society and ACEB. The idea of an equal sharing in the costs of the project indicated a change of approach and of dependence on God for the success of the project. There were no financial or material resources in sight!

So ACEB made a proposal to the two partners, the Bible Society of Togo and SIL Togo-Benin. This proposal had two propositions which defined the responsibilities of ACEB, and that of the partners, in the translation of the Old Testament.

ACEB's responsibilities for the Old Testament project

- ACEB is the initiator of the project for the translation of the Old Testament into the Bassar (Ncham) language.
- ACEB is responsible for the planning of the project and will determine the objectives at each stage of the project.

- ACEB will look for partners who will support the project for translating the Old Testament.

- ACEB will take responsibility for the good management of the funds allocated by the partners to achieve the objectives of the project.

- ACEB will report regularly on the progress of the project and give financial reports of the different stages of the project.

- ACEB will supervise responsibly the personnel assigned by the partners for service in the project.

- ACEB will sign a memorandum of understanding with its partners as soon as possible to forestall any possible changes during the execution of the project.

- ACEB will do as much as possible year by year to increase the effective participation of the local Church in the realisation of the translation of the Old Testament.

Responsibilities of ACEB's partners in the project for translating the Old Testament

- The partners will play their part in the project according to the call they have received from God.

- The status of each partner will be decided by ACEB according to their contribution to the project.

- The conditions each partner must fulfil will be determined by their responsibilities towards the project.
- The partners will offer their services to ACEB in relation to planning, budgets and supervision of the project.
- The partners will make their transfers into ACEB's bank account at the agreed times, until the budget which was voted for each year for the translation of the Old Testament has been met.

A plan of action was prepared by ACEB and submitted to two partners, the Bible Society of Togo, and SIL Togo-Benin.

Aim of the project to translate the Old Testament into Bassar (Ncham).

Strategy to promote the project with the churches and with partners, to mobilise people who can be of help to the project, and to look for potential financial partners.

Activities Translation, training of the translators, revision of the translation, checking the translation, and testing the translation with native speakers.

Beneficiaries The Bassar people in Togo and in Ghana.

Resources for the work Finances, equipment, (Word processors, printers, translation manuals) and an office where the translation team can work.

Personnel Translators (Samuel Nabine, Kpapou Laré, Samuel Kpagheri), keyboarder (Gbati Nabine), Coordinator-Exegete (Napo Poidi), Translation consultants from the Bible Society and SIL.

Expected result The Bible in Bassar (Ncham), one without the Apocrypha for the Protestants and one with the Apocrypha for the Catholics.

Number of verses translation of 20 verses per day for narrative texts.

Length of time for the project January 1995 to December 2006.

Contributions expected from the partners :

The Bible Society 50% of the salaries for the three translators and the keyboarder, equipment and office supplies for the project, the cost of publishing the translation, a translation consultant in the person of Dr. Ettien Koffi N'da.

SIL Togo-Benin Translation Consultant Sheila Crunden, Coordinator- Exegete Napo Poidi, and a financial contribution towards the project.

ACEB will be the employer of the translators, the keyboarder, and the personnel associated with the translation office in Bassar. It will provide an office for the translation team, and also cover the costs of training the translators in Biblical Hebrew in Israel, the reviewers from the churches, and the people to test the translation.

The local Church was taken into account in the realisation of this new project. This constitutes a source of pride, even if the participation of the local church, which was supposed to be 50% of the salaries of the translators, was difficult to realise. This certainly created an obstacle to be overcome for the translators and their families at times during the project. For example, during three successive years the translators worked without any part of their salary coming from the Association. Happily the contributions from partners like Wynet in England, and personal friends of the team members, more or less filled this hole.

The translation was supposed to start in January 1995. But it did not start until 1996, when the translators received training in the principles of translation, first in Lomé and then in Cotonou. The financial responsibility for the translators' training was left to the churches in Bassar. They surprised everybody when they found enough money to send two of the translators, Kpapou Laré and Samuel Kpagheri, to the Ivory Coast, and to the Home for Bible Translators (HBT) in Jerusalem in Israel, between 1997 and 1998. This preparation was a wonderful contribution to the Old Testament translation project in Ncham.

At the time, SIL Togo-Benin did not have a translation consultant sufficiently experienced to supervise a translation of the Old Testament. A delegation from ACEB made the journey to Lomé three times to discuss the project with the Bible Society of Togo. The first visit was made on 16th December 1993 by a delegation consisting of the secretary, Nadjombé Makou, the treasurer, Father Davis Mekkattuparambil, the translator Samuel Nabine, and the keyboarder Pierre Nabine, to present the Old Testament translation project to them, and discuss the expectations of the potential partners. On 3rd January 1994, a report approving this first meeting was addressed to the Bassar team by David Lantam Nabine, assistant to the Translation Consultant, Dr. Ettien Koffi N'da, on his behalf, and that of Amaté Atayi (the director of the Bible Society of Togo) Dr. Krijn van der Jagt and Dr. John Ellington of UBS, as follows:

To the Bassar team:

Dear Brothers in Christ,

It was a real pleasure to meet you on 16th December to discuss your project for translating the Old Testament. I hope you are still wanting to go ahead with this project. I was very pleased to see that you have thought through very carefully what you want to do. The aims of your association are witness to it. I hope that the overview which we made together of the conditions for working together have not discouraged you. I will briefly remind you of the important points raised at our meeting:

The copyright of the New Testament and the Old Testament : Since UBS does not hold the copyright for the New Testament, it will be necessary for you to obtain permission to use the texts of the New Testament, and eventually put them together with the Old Testament in order to make a whole Bible. For this purpose, I am sending you the forms for copyright in case you decide to do the Old Testament with us.

Qualified personnel : You must have at least two full-time translators, a maximum of three. It is also necessary to have an Exegete-Coordinator for the project, and a keyboarder with computer skills. The level of education required by UBS for translators is as follows:

- have the Bac
- have done at least two years at a seminary, either Protestant or Catholic

- have at least a rudimentary knowledge of Hebrew (for the Old Testament) and of Greek (for the New Testament)

Finances : UBS requires that a salary according to the level of education be paid to the translation personnel. For this, UBS is ready to contribute up to 50% of the finances for the project. In addition to that, UBS is ready to put quality equipment at the disposition of your team: computers, printers, disks, paper, and desks, if needed. The cost of the final printing will be entirely underwritten by UBS.

A word about the UBS's vision : The Bible Society is a Christian ministry devoted to putting the Word of God at the disposition of people in the language they understand best. To achieve this, they subsidise translation work in hundreds of languages throughout the world. UBS works with all Christian churches, and encourages translation where all the Christian denominations collaborate. Our desire is that your team should reflect the ecumenical character required by UBS.

In the expectation of a fruitful collaboration, please receive my best wishes for the year 1994.

Your brother in Christ,

Ettien Koffi N'da, Translation Consultant with UBS for Benin and Togo.

A second meeting for orientation to the principles of UBS was planned to enable the consultant Dr. Ettien Koffi N'da to better understand ACEB's perspectives. It took place on 12th

April 1994, again at the office of the Bible Society of Togo in Lomé. Here is an extract of the report sent on 20th April 1994 by the translation consultant:

> I want here to give you some more orientation and also seek to understand certain things myself.
>
> As you know, we at the Bible Society believe as you do that the translation of the Bible is above all a spiritual work, and will always be so. It is true that we insist on academic qualifications, but at the same time we know that it is the Holy Spirit who enlightens! Nevertheless, we don't underestimate the contribution of academic and theological training. I hope that the candidates you propose have the qualifications which I mentioned in one of my earlier letters. If not, it will be necessary to look for other candidates, or to enable them to obtain the necessary qualifications.
>
> When I read the page entitled 'the contributions expected from the partners', I saw that you expected UBS to pay 300,000 CFA francs a month for each of the three translators. Since I told you that UBS will pay half of the cost of the salaries, your report suggests to me that you expect to pay at least 200,000 CFA francs a month to each translator! If this is the case, the salary is too high. But if this is not the case, UBS alone cannot undertake the whole financial responsibility for the project. I want to remind you that UBS is ready to contribute 50% of the cost, once the project has been accepted by our headquarters in Nairobi.
>
> Concerning the consultants, I see that you have written that both UBS and SIL will provide you

with consultants. Even though UBS cooperates closely with SIL, a UBS project cannot have two or more consultants other than those of UBS. This means that you cannot have consultants from UBS and SIL for the Bassar project at the same time. What generally happens is that the SIL representative is the coordinator for the project. This person is responsible for planning the project, and for the exegetical work before and during the translation. But the final exegetical work, that is, checking the quality of the translated text, is the responsibility of UBS. Generally too, as often happens in our region, the translators do not know the Biblical languages, so the coordinator from SIL, or from any other mission, is required to have learnt these languages.

I see that you plan to begin in January 1995. It is good to have a starting date. But I think that from UBS' point of view, this date is too soon. First of all, it will be necessary to fulfil certain administrative formalities in Lomé and in Nairobi. It is when Nairobi has approved the project that a budget can be allocated for it. For my part I think that it will probably be in 1995-6 that we will hopefully find the money for the Bassar project.

Again, thank you for the excellent preparatory work which you have done; it is excellent and I hope to work with you in the preparation for this project. It will be a real joy for me to work with you because you are an association which is well-organised, and which knows precisely the objective you want to attain. May God bless your efforts.

With brotherly greetings in the Lord,
Dr. Ettien Koffi N'da

A third meeting with the consultant Dr. Ettien Koffi N'da took place on 23rd June 1995, this time in Cotonou where he was based. It was led by Emmanuel Ditone, the new Secretary of ACEB, and by Father Davis Mekkattuparambil, Gbati Nabine, and Father Olivier Djabaré. As a result of this meeting, it was decided that the the translators Kpapou Laré and Samuel Nabine (who was replaced by Samuel Kpagheri because of his academic level) should take part in an introductory course in Biblical Hebrew offered by Julie Bentinck of SIL in Bouaké, in Ivory Coast, in July 1997. This introductory course in Biblical Hebrew would prepare the two translators for an intensive six-month course in Biblical Hebrew from October 1997 at the Home for Bible Translators (HBT) in Jerusalem; this would be the first time the course would be held for African translators. The other members of the Old Testament translation team in Ncham were Samuel Labanté Nabine (translator), Napo Jeremy Poidi (exegetical co-ordinator), and Dr. Ettien Koffi N'da (translation consultant).

These meetings between ACEB and UBS were concluded by the signature of an agreement which recognised the Bible Society as having the responsibility for the translation of the Old Testament into Bassar, under the supervision of the Translation Consultant Dr. Ettien Koffi N'da. Three years after the beginning of the project, he was succeeded by three other consultants from UBS who checked the texts which had been translated into Ncham. They were Dr. John Ellington, Dr. Krijn van der Jagt, and Dr. Joachim Somé. Dr Somé was the consultant who checked the quality of most of the books of the Old Testament translated into Ncham.

The last phase of the project would be the translation of the deuterocanonical books, which was a requirement of the Catholic Church in return for its participation in Old Testament translation. With the translation of the deuterocanonical books (or the Apocrypha), two versions of the Bible would be available in the Ncham language: one version without the Apocrypha for the Protestants, and the other which included the deuterocanonical books for the Catholics.

The New Testament was revised in its entirety by the translators and the exegetical coordinator, and so the process of translating the two Testaments was completed.

Trials experienced during the translation of the Old Testament

It was expected that the project would take 10 years, from 1997 to 2007, but in fact it took 15 years, from 1997 to 2012. The team met many obstacles during their work to complete the project of translating the Old Testament. We will mention only a few of them: first, the death of the translator Christophe Kpapou Laré in 2008, leaving a widow with five children; then there was the illness of Samuel Labanté Nabine which left him handicapped; there was the serious car accident which took place between Bassar and Kara and which nearly cost the life of translator Samuel Tinindjotobe Kpagheri, while he was transporting the final version of the translation of the Ncham Old Testament to the SIL Centre in Kara. The last phase of the translation saw many financial difficulties. The translation team, now reduced to two members, (Samuel Kpagheri and Daniel Seyi) had many testing times before they were able to complete the translation of the Old Testament. Nevertheless, the translators persevered. With the help of the Coordinator and the President of ACEB, and also the support given by the Director of the Bible Society of Togo, Pastor Wolanyo Amegah, they were able to finish the revision of the New Testament in September 2012. The two Testaments (Old and New) of the Bible in Ncham were put together and were published as the Bible in the Bassar (Ncham) language, to the great joy of the local Church and the Bassar populations of Togo and of Ghana.

The contributions of the Bible Society of Togo, of SIL Togo-Benin, and more modestly that of Wycliffe-Togo, plus the contributions of ACEB and of Wynet, their partner from Wycliffe-UK, and from our Swiss friends, are inestimable. But the prize belongs to the team of translators who sacrificed themselves so that these two projects were completed with the help of God.

Chapter 4

An open door for a new translation project

During a visit to the village of Sassanou, the Lord opened our eyes to the need to translate the Holy Scriptures into the Igo language. During our stay in the village, Honorine discovered that the Christians mixed Biblical values with their ancestral culture and beliefs. She realised that this could be the result of not fully understanding the Biblical texts in the Ewe language, which was used in church. Honorine was convinced that a translation of the Holy Scriptures into the Igo language would shed light and enable the mother-tongue speakers of the Igo language to have a better understanding of the message of the Bible.

But there was a barrier to the project of translating the Holy Scriptures into Igo: would the local church among the Bogo people, and the people as a whole, support a translation project in their language ? This barrier was removed when the leaders of the local Church and those of the traditional beliefs of the Bogo people decided to give their full support to the project. The Regent of the village of Illogo said at the time: "The translation project in the Igo language is like a sycamore on which the little Bogo people will climb in order to see Jesus."

A second barrier to be overcome was that the Igo language was not yet written. Honorine decided to undertake linguistic research into Igo, which was her mother tongue. This opportunity opened the way for a new project to translate the New Testament into the Igo language (also known as Ahlon, a name given to them by neighbouring peoples).

The Bogo, a distinctive people

Igo is spoken today by a population of about 7,300 in the Canton of the Bogo, to the west of the Danyi plateau. The Bogo are a small people-group in Togo, living principally in five villages: Bogo, Sassanou (also called Illogo), Tinipé, Dénu, and Awunadjassi. They are ruled by village chiefs, and a Canton chief. The illiteracy rate among the Bogo is estimated to be 75%. The majority of the illiterates are women, who represent 60% of the population. The principal economic activity among the Bogo is agriculture, based on the cultivation of coffee. The canton has three weekly markets, where fruit and vegetables, cereals and tubers are bought and sold. The production of manufactured goods is very underdeveloped.

The Bogo travelled with a large people-group, the Ewe, from ancient Egypt, passing through the country which is now called Nigeria. Some people say that the Bogo are distant cousins of the Ibo people of Nigeria. According to a study we made, about 40% of Igo words are derived from the Ibo language.

From a social point of view, each village has a primary school. The canton has only two secondary schools, for general studies. The college is about 25 km from the last Bogo village, and the regional hospital is 60 km away. However, there is a health centre in the principal town of the prefecture of Danyi, and dispensaries in the villages. The roads which lead to the villages are impassable in the rainy season.

It was in the beauty of these mountains and valleys, among one of the most hospitable of peoples, that we spent the happiest days of our ministry in Bible translation with our four children.

Linguistic research in Igo

On 2nd November 1991, we were officially assigned in the village of Illogo to start a translation and literacy project in the Igo language. Before we arrived, our SIL Togo-Benin branch had obtained the necessary authorisation to carry out linguistic research and Bible translation from the government ministry under whose auspices we worked. Until that time, no advanced linguistic research had been done on the Igo language, apart from the work begun by Hiné, a German linguist.

While we were working there, we benefitted greatly from the support of the Paramount Chief of the Bogo, Onde Yao Adoboli Gassou IV. The following were our close collaborators from among the Bogo: Koffi Banissi, Abotchi Kokou, Evouké Anani, Wolako Dolagbénou, and Komlan Goka, who became the first supervisor of the literacy programme in Igo.

Our team continued its linguistic research and study of the Igo language which resulted in a systematic description of Igo.[1] In addition to that, the Igo project team received spir-

---

[1] Massanvi Honorine Gblem-Poidi (1995). "Description systématique de l'igo". Thèse de Doctorat Nouveau Régime. Grenoble: Université Stendhal.

itual training for more than a year through Bible studies and intercessory prayer for the Bogo people and the Igo project.

The literacy programme in the Igo language was launched on the 25th of August 1992, and in particular it was also the day when the dedication of the very first reading primer in Igo took place. 300 copies were printed of this manual, which taught how to read and write the Igo language. The dedication ceremony for the Igo primer took place in the large Presbyterian Church of Togo, in the village called Bogo. All the important and influential people from among the Bogo were present: the Cantonal Chief Gassou IV, the village chiefs, important people from all the villages, pastors from the Canton and native Bogo pastors, catechists, deacons and deaconesses, the committee of the traditional festival of Onana, the education committee of the Canton, and teachers from the primary and secondary schools. SIL Togo-Benin was represented by its director, Eric Bartels, and assistant director, Dave MacNeil. Many Bogo people from the five villages also came.

Following this ceremony of dedication, a cantonal committee of 25 members was formed to supervise the translation movement among the Bogo.

On 31st of August 1992, the Cantonal Committee met for the first time at the home of the Cantonal chief, Gassou IV, in the village of Bogo, to elect the officers of the committee and establish the process by which literacy teachers would be chosen, two for each village. These volunteers would follow the very first course for training literacy teachers in Igo.

The following were the members of the committee : Kano Atsou (president), Ekumli Goka (vice president), Azunu Ata (secretary), Elolo Kofi (assistant secretary), Mrs. Afua Ata (treasurer), and Moise Gadagbé (assistant treasurer). The other members of the Cantonal Committee, among whom were leaders of the first churches planted among the Bogo, would be advisers to the Igo project.

From 7-12th September 1992, our linguistic research team organised a training course for literacy teachers in the village of Illogo. In all, 17 participants were trained. From 16-17th September 1992, the Cantonal Committee undertook a tour of the whole Canton to inform and encourage people to become literate in Igo. Our co-workers took part in this tour, which began in the village of Awunadjassi, continued through the villages of Dénou, Tinipé and Bogo, and ended in Illogo. Between 5-8th October 1992, the first classes were opened in all the villages. Twenty days after the start of the classes (that is, on 28th October), the teachers had their first meeting to report on how the classes were progressing. Their report showed that over the whole Canton, 123 people had signed up and were attending the classes regularly.

At the end of each week during the time the classes were taking place, the literacy teachers met to discuss how the classes were progressing. The aim of these meetings was to train the teachers by looking for solutions to the problems they met during the classes, and also to encourage them in their work.

The sociopolitical situation in the country at the time was dominated by a general strike. The primer was not selling well, because economic activities in the Canton were paralysed. But attendance at the classes was growing strongly. The civil servants on strike had all returned to their villages of origin. This was an opportunity to be seized by the Igo project. The supervisor of the literacy programme and his team decided to reorganise the sale and distribution of the primers, orthography booklets and reading booklets in Igo.

Then, from January to March 1993, all the personnel of the Igo project were mobilised for a reading and writing course in the five principal villages of the Canton, aimed at the Bogo who were literate in French. The length of the course was one week per village. The results of this action were spectacular. After five weeks of training, 149 Bogo literate in French had learnt to read their own Igo language. Among those who took the course, many were from Lomé, the capital of Togo. The others came from towns such as Kpalimé, Atakpamé and other towns where the general strike had paralysed every activity and the sociopolitical troubles had made everyone return to their native village. The general strike had positively encouraged the Igo literacy work.

Revival among the Bogo

During this period, the Cantonal Committee took action which would be decisive for the literacy project among the Bogo. The Committee held two important meetings in the village of Dénou, on 6th February 1993 and then a month later in March. The meeting held in Dénou enabled the members of the Cantonal Committee who were present (15 people), with the addition of several literacy teachers, to reflect on the results of the literacy programme in Igo. This reflection indicated that the results of this programme would be, among other things, the ability to read and write Igo. This would mean real autonomy for the Bogo people who live among other larger people groups. The Bogo would be able to make their own contribution to national reconstruction, and the socio-economic development of the people could begin. The Igo language would be used in audio-visual media. The translation of the Bible into Igo would make access to the Word of God and to salvation in Christ easier, and the it would be possible to translate songs and other literature, which is useful for the people's development.

To accomplish its mission effectively, the Cantonal Committee had only one strategy in mind: that of the involvement of the local church and the Bogo community. Their intention was to act with the help of the Holy Spirit and by faith. They would take the work to heart and intercede for it. They would have frequent meetings to seek solutions for the progress of the project, and work in close cooperation with the literacy teachers. They would hold at least one meeting a month in each village in turn, to support the literacy volunteers by all means locally available and to help the village committees in their work. They would make periodic tours of the villages and farming communities in the Canton to encourage them in their work, and to mobilise resources. The literacy programme was an instrument of development. It would also help solve the critical problems facing the people. These were social problems such as common illnesses in the area, drunkenness, drugs, and immorality, and spiritual problems such as necromancy and idolatry which resulted in witchcraft.

Conscious of their limitations, the members of the Cantonal Committee relied on prayer and intercession to enable them to lift the heavy burden of challenges facing the Bogo people. They decided to establish a day of prayer and intercession in the Canton for the literacy and translation project in Igo. Every third Wednesday of the month was set aside for this spiritual event in the churches of the Canton throughout the duration of the Igo project. The Wednesday prayer meeting would be followed by a collection of money from those who were willing to support the translation of the Holy Scriptures into Igo, and literacy work in the whole Canton. This would be the contribution of the Bogo people towards the project for translating the Bible and for literacy in the Igo language.

At this time, a series of books was produced in Igo, in particular the Igo literacy primer, *Bogo éku* (*Traditional Bogo Tales*), *Ijolué ni olo* (*Bogo Riddles and Proverbs*), *Anɔbi ulu ulu* (*Bogo Stories*), portions of the Gospel of Mark, and a manual of Igo orthography.

There was a total craze in the villages for learning Igo. At the time, we witnessed a revival of prayer, especially in the parish churches. There was record attendance in the churches on Sundays. It was at that time an event took place which made its mark on our village and the rest of the Canton. In September 1999, a soothsayer who was an eminent personality of the traditional religion in our village, accepted Jesus Christ as his Lord and Saviour because of our testimony. He then wanted to know what he should do with his many idols, now that he had received the Lord. We suggested that with his consent, we would organise an evangelistic meeting in the village square on a Sunday afternoon to burn his fetishes in the presence of witnesses, and we would take the opportunity to preach the Gospel of Jesus Christ to everybody. When the day came, we piled the fetishes in a heap in the square, in the presence of a large number of curious villagers. After a time of singing praises and prayer to God, and after the testimony of the new convert, the evangelist Issifou of the Assemblies of God, sent by the church for the occasion, preached the Word of God from the Bible to the assembled company. After that, we set fire to the heap of fetishes and other undesirable objects. This event spread fear among the population that day. Everyone expected reprisals from the spirits against us after the ceremony. But the protection of the Lord Jesus Christ was clearly over us, and over all those who believed in him. After that there was a movement of the Holy Spirit among many of the villagers who gave their lives to Jesus Christ, about 80 people. A Christian community had been born.

God speaks Igo

The translation of the Holy Scriptures into the Igo language began with the books of the Gospel of Jesus Christ. This resulted in the publication in 2004 of the four books, Matthew, Mark, Luke and John, in one volume. Today the Bogo people can rejoice in the fact that the New Testament in the Igo language is henceforth available for every Ogo[2] person in the language of his heart. The translation team, coordinated by Honorine, finished the work in 2013 with the typesetting of the Igo translation, under the supervision of two computer technicians, George Mbeck and Brian Anderson of CABTAL (Wycliffe Cameroon), in Yaounde. The final version of the New Testament was printed in South Korea, to the great joy of the Bogo people. An audio recording of the Igo New Testament will also be made. This Igo New Testament was dedicated in May 2015, the same weekend as the funeral of the Paramount Chief of the Bogo, who died shortly after the arrival of the New Testament in the port of Lome. When he heard the news, he said: "Now my people can understand the Word of God better, because it is now available in Igo, our mother tongue. This New Testament will contribute not only to the salvation of the people, but also to the saving of our language." The Paramount Chief of the Bogo gave himself to the Lord before he died.

The road has been long, because the Igo project saw a period of slow-down between 1998 and 2006 due to a lack of adequate support for the project. A characteristic of the Igo

---

[2] 'Ogo' is the singular of 'Bogo' and means a person of the Bogo ethnic and linguistic group.

translation project is that it was a project of the local church and of the people. It did not receive external support from the SIL financial system. The only exception was a contribution from the friends of Father Marian Schwark of the OCDI, who at a particular point in time gave a breath of fresh air to the Igo literacy project.

The realisation of this translation of the New Testament into Igo had several different aspects, namely: the different phases of the translation, the way the translation team worked, the different workers in the team for the translating the New Testament, the training given to those workers, and the translation consultants.

The phases of the translation The translation of the Igo New Testament went through three phases with a pause between each:

> **Phase 1** the translation of the four books of the Gospel of Jesus Christ, followed by their publication in one volume, then the translation and checking of the Acts of the Apostles and the Epistle to the Romans.
>
> **Phase 2** the translation of the Epistles from I Corinthians to James.
>
> **Phase 3** the translation of the Epistles from I Peter to Revelation.

The method the team followed The method followed by the team went through the following stages:

> **Stage 1** The translators made a first draft and typed it.
>
> **Stage 2** The manuscript was read by a team of literacy teachers to check the orthography, and the clarity and naturalness of the style.

Stage 3 The corrected text was sent to groups of reviewers in the five villages of the Canton. A revision of the translation was made by the reviewers from each village met together in one place.

Stage 4 The corrections were made at the same time as a back- translation into French so that the text could be checked by a translation consultant.

Stage 5 The checking of the translation was done by a consultant who worked with a team of four people: two reviewers chosen by turn, and two translators, one of whom was Honorine, the coordinator of the project. At each checking session, the members who took part in the checking with the coordinator and the keyboarder were changed. The other members of the team were chosen from those who had taken part in the translation or in the back-translation.

The workers in the Igo translation team The Igo translation team had three groups of workers:

The first group was that of the translators. They were people who had been trained in the principles of Bible translation to produce the first draft of the translation into Igo. They were Honorine Gblem-Poidi, Atta Azunu, Kudzo Agbo, Augustin Folly-Katse, and Abotsi Kokou.

The second group was the reading committee composed of members of the language committee who had mastered the Igo writing system and were given the responsibility of re-reading the text and putting it into good shape. They were Ofu Goka, Wolako Dolagbenou, Koffi Bothe, Robert Evouke, Cephas Kodzogan, Anani Evouke, Gabriel Abotsi Gameti, and Banissi Koffi.

Last of all, the third group was composed of the reviewers. They were a team of three people per village, one church leader and two literacy teachers, which made a total of fifteen people in all: Hélène Etse-Gblem, Mana Gloria Atsu, Kayi Vovomele, Koffi Bothe, Robert Evouke, Cephas Kodzogan, Anani Evouke, Augustine Gameti, Banissi Koffi, Bertine Edzetse, Kudzo Agbo, Grace Edéfoe, Augustin Katse, Rev. Seth Séwonou and Rev. Cephas Douamenyo.

The training given to the workers in the translation team

The translators all received the standard training given by SIL in the principles of translation and in exegesis. They all worked under the supervision of the coordinator of the project and the translation consultants. The reading committee also received training in the Igo writing system, and the reviewers were given training in how to revise the translation of Biblical texts. The final revision sessions brought together all the reviewers from the five principal villages for a whole week or more. These sessions provided opportunities to increase the capability of each member of the translation team.

The computer technicians of SIL Togo-Benin in Kara, Bonaventure Ayite and Eric Esse also made an important contribution to the training of the members of the team, especially with the Paratext programme and in other areas of information technology.

The translation consultants Five Bible translation consultants brought their expertise to the checking of the New Testament texts translated into Igo: they were Sheila Crunden, Tony Pope, Hans Hoddenbagh, Antoine Yegbe and Pierre Barassounon. Pierre did the final checking of the New Testament with the Igo team in Parakou, northern Benin.

The development of the Igo language and literacy

The Igo language is the basic cultural tool of the Bogo community, a means of communication and exchange, and at the same time an instrument for mastering the knowledge which is indispensable for progress and for development in all its aspects for the Bogo community, which lives beside its large neighbour, the Ewe.

The development of the Igo language and literacy are essential elements for encouraging the development of the people and the Canton of the Bogo. Access to education is much easier when it is done through their mother tongue, Igo. It is very difficult and at the same time discouraging to learn the language of wider communication which one does not know or knows only a little. This is moreover one important reason which explains the high rate of illiteracy everywhere in Africa. The fact that people are expected to learn to read and write a language which they do not speak from childhood is a factor which discourages them from learning to read. If people learn to read in their own language, that increases the rate of success, because they are learning in a language which they know and love.

Once the Bogo can read in Igo, they will have access to material with teaching on various subjects, such as the fight against HIV/AIDS, Ebola, hygiene, and other books about health, agriculture, and general knowledge, translated into Igo. Literature appropriate to the needs of the Bogo people can be developed by the Bogo themselves, those who have learnt to read and write their own language. Knowing how to read and write in Igo enables the Bogo to appreciate their cultural heritage and affirm their identity.

For some people, learning to read in their own language will open the door to learning a language of wider communication in the country. In this way they will also be able to increase their knowledge thanks to all the information available in this other language.

Learning to read and write your mother tongue is very important, especially in nursery and primary school. It is important that children should be taught their mother tongue in their first three years at primary school. This stimulates children to learn to read and write because it is their mother tongue and they understand it. In this way they will be able to learn other languages more easily when they are a little older.

Chapter 5

The birth of Wycliffe-Togo

The translation of the Bible into our mother tongues in Togo is a gift from God. The stakes are high, given that the future of the Church in Africa is played out on the field of the proclaimed Word. Already false prophets and false teachers have appeared and are trying to win ground in the country. Added to this spiritual climate is a troubled sociopolitical situation which continues to this day. This situation, let us remember, is a consequence of the 'east wind'[1] of democracy which began to blow in francophone Africa when the French colonial power decided that it should be so, after the French president François Mitterrand's famous speech at the Baule[2].

---

[1] 'The east wind' is the conflict between the Western powers (the USA and Europe) and those of the East (China and the then Soviet Union).
[2] It was at the Conference at the Baule, in 1990, that President François Mitterrand of France had encouraged all the African countries to embrace democracy and multi-partyism.

At the beginning of 1992, just before a serious sociopolitical crisis in the form of a general strike[3] took place in Togo, the Togolese Church took note of the efforts being made by the agencies for Bible translation in the country, and decided to become involved in this domain of language development, the translation of the Holy Scriptures and literacy in the mother tongues of Togo.

On 2nd April 1992, we organised an important meeting at the Hôtel du Golfe in Lomé which brought together key people belonging to twelve ethnic and linguistic groups in Togo: Akposso, Bassar, Ewe, Gangam, Igo, Ifè, Kabyè, Mina, Moba, Nawdem, Anoufo and Tem.

The aim of this meeting was to share the vision for translation, literacy and the promotion of local languages. At the end of the meeting, an appropriate strategy for the Togolese context was put in writing and shared with close partners in September, and then presented at the SIL regional conference for Africa. This was held in Nairobi, Kenya, in October of the same year.

"If the vision seem slow, wait for it." (Habakkuk 2:3b)

The vision received consisted of forming an agency within each ethnic and linguistic group in Togo and beyond with the responsibility for creating an appropriate orthography for the local language; and to promote the orthography by making it an instrument for written communication, teaching and mass education, with the goal of lasting development for the people who speak it.

---

[3] The general strike called by the political opposition in Togo lasted for nine months.

Next, the aim would be to make the Holy Scriptures, and also all literature suitable for Christian teaching, available to each people-group in their mother tongue, to fulfil what was written by the prophet Habakkuk: "The earth will be filled with the knowledge of the glory of the LORD as the waters cover the sea." (Habakkuk 2:14)

The strategy adopted was to begin to build from the bottom up, by putting into place local structures suitable for the context of each ethnic and linguistic group (local organisation, LO), then by putting into place regional structures (regional organisation, RO), and finally by establishing a national structure (Wycliffe Togo, WT). The regional and national structures would have a coordinating function.

Also, seven linguistic regions were identified throughout the territory of Togo, following a genetic grouping of languages: Gurma A, Gurma B, Gurunsi A, Gurunsi B, Kwa, Volta-Mono and Gbe. The by-laws of the national structure were drawn up and the different stages for establishing the local organisations were worked out.

"The righteous will live by his faith" (Habakkuk 2:4b NIV 1973)

Eight years later, at the beginning of the year 2000, the vision had developed into specific Bible translation projects. Local associations for the promotion of the mother tongue, literacy, and the translation and promotion of the Holy Scriptures had been formed, and, in 1998, a steering committee was constituted to set up the national structure. The principal people in this movement working with the Steering Committee were, to mention only a few, Professor Lantam Seyi, Liberty Aziadekey,

Michel Dagoh, Dr. Konrad Dogba, Frank Gbedey, and Father Marian.

The leaders of the Council of Christian Churches of Togo (CCCT), and the Federation of Togolese Evangelicals (FTE) gave their blessing to the beginning of the Wycliffe mission in Togo, in order to involve the Church in the movement for Bible Translation and literacy, to build up the Church, and to further the development of the ethnic and linguistic communities in Togo.

In 1999, the wider family of Wycliffe organisations throughout the world adopted a vision called Vision 2025. This aims to begin a translation project for every language which needs it, by the year 2025.

The conditions had come together for founding a Wycliffe mission in Togo for the translation of the Bible. Wycliffe Togo saw the light of day during a founding conference held on 28-29th April 2000 at the SIL Centre in Lomé.

The evolution of the vision

The path of the Bible translation movement between 1992 and 2000 was strewn with obstacles. It had been necessary to pull down, uproot and rebuild (Jeremiah 1:10) in order to transform the churches' mentality toward the mission of Bible translation. The aim of the meeting on 2nd of April had been first of all to awaken the conscience of key people who spoke the twelve principal languages of the country. These influential people belonged to different Christian denominations. Their mission was to inform and stimulate the interest of their church leaders, and in particular the movers and shakers among their own people, and to give them information which would be useful for setting in motion a movement for Bible translation in Togo.

The programme for the meeting on 2nd of April was prepared for this purpose. Specialists from SIL described the major themes of Bible translation: linguistic research (Jann Russell), translation (Marcel Gasser), and literacy (Bob de Craene). But the accent was placed in particular on an aspect often left to one side, the role of the local Church in the realisation of the translation of the Bible into a given language (Napo Poidi).

This meeting enabled us to lay a solid foundation for the Bible translation movement in Togo. However, we needed to convince our partners, in particular my expatriate colleagues in SIL Togo-Benin, that the vision of the newborn movement was well-grounded. Everyone's collaboration would be needed if the objectives of the Bible translation movement were to be realised.

Seven months elapsed after this meeting. In October 1992, the vision of the movement for Bible translation in Togo was at last shared with the Executive Committee of SIL Togo-Benin, of which I was a member, during its regular meeting in Kara. After this presentation, the Director of SIL Togo-Benin sent a message to call and motivate all the members in Togo and in Benin to support the vision of the movement. Here is the text of the message:

> To all Branch members
>
> Date: 14th October 1992
>
> From Eric Bartels, Director
> CC: U. Bukies, EC Chairman N.Poidi (Lome); File
> Re: enclosed reports on Togo NBTO.
> Ref: EB/pp/92/516

Dear Colleagues,

Greetings to each of you. As you have seen from reading your copy of the most recent EC meetings, Napo Poidi presented to the EC his vision for an NBTO (National Bible Translation Organisation) in Togo.

Napo's vision involves the creation of local translation and literacy organisations in each language group. The local Associations would then group into regional and national federations.

EC greatly appreciated Napo's presentation, and requested that the Admin sends copies to all the branch members.

The EC minutes state:

> 'The EC is grateful for what Napo has shared, and is in general agreement with his vision. The EC encourages Napo and the administration to further pursue these ideas together with other nationals as well as SIL members. It is our desire to involve as many nationals as possible. The EC further invites the branch membership to consider this vision and pray for the Lord's guidance in implementing it.'

Following up on this, I am happy to send each of you the enclosed pages, and would encourage each of you to read them, to pray about what is presented there, to discuss any questions you may have with Napo, and to consider carefully what your role may be in furthering these developments.

Yours in Christ,

Eric.

You will find below the presentation of the vision of the movement for Bible translation which Napo made to the Executive Committee of SIL Togo-Benin (EC):

Mr. Chairman, and members of the Executive Committee of SIL Togo-Benin,

Dear Colleagues,

> "A nation without God's guidance is a nation without order.
> Happy is the man who keeps God's law!" (Proverbs 29:18 TEV)

On Saturday 4th January 1992, the Bassar people received its New Testament. Glory be to God!

For the SIL Togo-Benin branch, it was the first New Testament in its history. For SIL in general, it was one more New Testament, another dedication and articles here and there. But, you will agree with me that this cannot be all there is for the Bible translation ministry to which we have been called among the peoples of Africa.

In coming to Wycliffe, then to SIL, we have all received from our Lord Jesus Christ the call and the vision to give to at least one people-group without the Bible the Word of God in the language they understand best. But to have a vision, even one coming from God, is not enough. We must also understand the meaning of that vision and act on it to save the people.

In Egypt, Pharoah also had a vision from God. It was the same for King Nebuchadnezzar of Babylon. In both cases, it was not enough to receive a vision from God; it was necessary to understand not only the vision but also the appropriate strategy from God for the fulfilment of the vision they had received (Genesis 41:25, Daniel 2:4).

In the two cases cited above, they had to seek out men of God, Joseph and Daniel, who had the Spirit of God and were able to understand and interpret the vision, and receive from God the strategy to be followed. Our Lord Jesus Christ has poured out this Spirit generously into our hearts (Titus 3:6-7), so that we should understand every biblical vision, in particular the one relating to the translation of the Bible, and to receive the strategy suitable for the situations concerned. So it is by faith in Jesus Christ that I share with you this new orientation for SIL.

The Bible was written for our instruction. To understand any vision from God, it is necessary to analyse it in the light of the Bible itself. The Church lives in the world today as though it were in two boxes, representing Egypt and Babylon. At the heart of these two principal stages which affected the life of the people of God, we find the ministry of the translation and diffusion of the Word of God, symbolised by:

1. The mission of Joseph in Egypt; that is, to pro-

vide food for the people faced with famine, and to allow God to make of Jacob a large nation in Goshen. This was followed by the mission of Moses and the journey from Egypt to the promised land.

2. The mission of Daniel, Joshua, Zerubbabel, Esther, Ezra and Nehemiah, which resulted in the return of God's people to the promised land and the restoration of the Temple in Jerusalem, and also the city wall.

This vision of the ministry of the Word of God cannot be applied today to every situation in the world. It is necessary to identify the different streams of development of the people of God, the Church, in each continent, region and sub-region, in every country and in every ethnic and linguistic group; the times and the boundaries of whose lands have been fixed by God, according to his Word, in order to reveal his Son to every person. In other words, we need to enter into the vision which God himself has of the ministry which we have the privilege and responsibility to exercise (Ps. 2:8, Matt. 24:14, Acts 17:26-31, Rev. 5).

When we follow closely the path Uncle Cam (William Cameron Townsend) took, that is exactly what he did. He put to one side his understanding of the nation state of Guatemala and of Spanish as the language of Guatemala, in order to consider the particular situation of an Indian tribe, the Cachiquel people and their mother tongue. It cannot be denied that the Church and people of Guatemala were in great need of the ministry of Bible distribution in Spanish which

William Cameron Townsend exercised. He aimed to make the Holy Scriptures acccessible to the Guatemalan people. But the situation in the country of Guatemala as a whole did not correspond to the particular situation of the Indian people in question. The church had not yet been established in the Cachiquel nation. This fact explains well the ministry which Uncle Cam accomplished among them. Nevertheless, one cannot copy this ministry, which was accomplished at a particular time in a particular context, in every situation without considering first whether it is appropriate.

In this way, the point of reference for the translation of the Bible is the local church. It is necessary to understand what this means. Local churches in the same country or continent will have different composition and maturity in different ethnic and linguistic groups. In every case, the notion of the local church is more than one Christian denomination. It embraces the totality of the Body of Christ in its doctrinal and ecclesiastic diversity as it has been planted in any given ethnic and linguistic community. (Matt. 28:19-20)

In Africa today, it is rare to find a people-group where there are no Christians or no church. In some ethnic and linguistic groups, the local church is still very small. It is like the family of Jacob in Egypt at the time of the Pharoahs. It needs spiritual food in order to grow. It needs to find space like a spiritual Goshen in order to expand. In this case, it needs servants like Joseph and later Moses, Joshua and Caleb, for its deliverance from

The evolution of the vision

Egypt and its entry into the promised land of Canaan.

On the other hand, in some ethnic and linguistic groups, the local church has grown and has a strong influence on its environment, to such an extent that one can even speak of a 'Christian ethnic group'. But because of sin within it, the local church needs to be purified and return to the light of the Word of God. In this case, the Church is figuratively in exile in Babylon. The ministries of men of God like Jeremiah, Daniel, Joshua, Zerubbabel, Esther, Ezra and Nehemiah are necessary to bring the people back to God and to the Word of his Son Jesus Christ. Here the builders and the prophets worked together (Jeremiah 1, Ezra 1:5, 5:2, 6:14; Haggai 2:4, Zechariah 4:6-7, Eph 4:11, I Cor.12).

Practically, all this requires the setting up of appropriate structures in the form of local autonomous ministries with the responsibility of translating the Bible, teaching literacy, and the promotion of an authentic gospel culture in each ethnic and linguistic group.

In a country like Togo, these local ministries will be headed by regional organisations responsible for questions of common interest, then by a federal ministry at a national level, a Wycliffe association with the responsibility for Bible translation, literacy and extending the influence of Gospel witness nationwide. (Matthew 5)

On a continental scale, the application of this strategy will imply a restructuring of each NBTO which is already established, and a redefinition of its relationship with SIL, carrying out their respective missions in the same country.

This profile which I have sketched in broad outline at local, regional and national levels gives us the appropriate strategy to carry out the biblical vision for translating the Holy Scriptures in our context today. The profile is conceived with the double purpose of the ministry of Bible translation in view:

1. To contribute to the spiritual edification of the church called out from each people-group, and to effective Christian witness, expanded through the use of the Holy Scriptures in the mother tongue.

2. To re-establish the worth of the basic culture of a people-group by linguistic research, by giving each language an adequate orthography, and by the application of research to different aspects of the social life of these people-groups.

Humbly submitted

Napo

This presentation of the vision was an important stage in the Bible translation movement in Togo and Benin.

But not everything was achieved at once. The development of the movement towards a Wycliffe association had to go through various stages: the formation of a steering committee to think through the creation of an organisation for Bible translation and literacy; gaining the support and cooperation of the leaders of churches and missions in Togo; the formation of an advisory committee of wise people from the Church in

Togo; the drawing up of by-laws suitable for Wycliffe organisations; the organisation of a founding congress to establish the administrative procedures of the association; the setting up of the procedure for obtaining official recognition of Wycliffe Togo by the Togolese government.

In 1992, Pierre Guy, Chair of the Committee of Wycliffe France, gave us his expertise in composing the by-laws for Wycliffe Togo. From 1998 onwards, the steering committee went through these by-laws with a fine toothcomb. Then they were revised by each partnering Church of this fledgling association, in order to reach the final version of the Wycliffe Togo association by-laws, which was presented to the founding congress.

The founding congress

The day after the celebration of Togo's 40 years of independence, the founding congress took place at last on the 28th April 2000, with a view to creating the Wycliffe Association for the Translation of the Bible and Literacy in Togo. The meetings covered two days, 28th and 29th April 2000. The guest of honour at the congress was an eminent personality, David Cummings, at the time the outgoing president of Wycliffe International. He had been the director of Wycliffe in his native Australia. At that time, Mr. Cummings was visiting Africa, Chad in particular, where his son was a missionary. He had accepted our invitation to come to Lomé to make a presentation about Wycliffe organisations during the the founding congress of the very first Wycliffe association in Africa. To be precise, there was already a Wycliffe association in South Africa at the time. However, it was attached to the European Region due to apartheid, the racial segregation which separated everything to do with whites from everything to do with blacks.

The choice of David Cummings, the ex-president of Wycliffe International, was supported by the director of SIL Togo-Benin at the time, Margrit Kuratli. We all wanted the new association to have the DNA of Wycliffe as a mission, and not the DNA of SIL. We were not disappointed in our expectations. President Cummings' presentation shone the light very clearly on Wycliffe organisations.

Mr. Cummings then continued his journey to Cotonou, where we took him to meet Barnabé and Eliane Mensah, and the leaders of churches in Benin, about the creation of another Wycliffe association.

The steering committee which had been given the responsibility of promoting the Wycliffe mission in Togo had done an excellent job of sharing the vision with church leaders, and with the two church federations, for more than two years between 1998 and 2000. For almost two years, this steering committee had met nearly every week, first in the flat at the SIL Centre in Lomé where my family was living, and then in the home of Michel and Florence Dagoh in Kégué, on the outskirts of Lomé, in order to make a distinction between Wycliffe and SIL Togo-Benin. This precaution was taken with the sole aim of making the movement for Bible translation leading to the creation of Wycliffe Togo authentically Togolese. The steering committee was composed of people from different walks of life, churches, languages and professions. Their work made it possible for the leaders of the Church in Togo, including the Catholic Church, and in particular the Society of the Divine Word (SVD) and the OCDI, represented by its director, Father Marian Schwark, to take on board the vision for Bible translation. Even though the movement for Bible translation was evangelical, the vision for making the Bible available to every people-group in its mother tongue had brought together all members of the Body of Christ in Togo. In this way, the movement for Bible translation had positioned itself as part of the Mission of God, which calls the Body of Christ to partake of the divine meal of his Word translated into each person's mother tongue around the table which He has laid.

This mobilisation of church leaders was instrumental for the birth of Wycliffe Togo. Every Church and institution represented at the founding Congress of 28-29 April 2000 had to send three delegates, and these had to be important people. The speaker chosen for the occasion was Rev. Jeoffree Tomtania from Calvary Temple in Lomé. The biblical text on which his message was based was taken from the Gospel of Matthew 9:37-38: "Then he said to his disciples, 'The harvest is plentiful but the workers are few. Ask the Lord of the harvest, therefore, to send out workers into his harvest field.'"

At the end of the founding congress, a Board of Directors made up of eleven members representing the churches and different insitutions was set up. Their mission was to be ambassadors sent to Wycliffe Togo by their respective churches in the Christian Council and the Federation of Evangelicals (FET), by the GBUST, Women's Ministries in Togo, and by the Bible Society of Togo. They were from different professions, and had different skills useful for the efficient running of Wycliffe Togo. An Executive Committee of six members with a director at its head was also in place some days after the founding congress. So from its foundation, the structure of Wycliffe Togo was created to fulfil the vision of mobilising the local Church in all its aspects to accomplish the translation of the Bible in Togo and elsewhere in Africa.

Developing partnership

The key to the making Wycliffe Togo's mission sustainable was the commitment of the local churches. These churches grasped the point very quickly. As a result they organised themselves so as to allow the young Wycliffe Togo to be introduced to each of them. To do that, they organised a missionary week in each Christian denomination in turn for the benefit of Wycliffe Togo. The programme began at Calvary Temple, the local church of the speaker at the founding congress of Wycliffe Togo, Rev. Jeoffree Tomtania, of the Assemblies of God in Togo. Then it was the turn of the Church of Pentecost in Togo, and after that the Baptist Convention of Togo, and so it continued.

The first missionary week enabled Wycliffe Togo to hold meetings with the men, the women, the youth, and finally with the whole church at Calvary Temple. There was a spontaneous freewill offering for Wycliffe Togo which came to 89,000 CFA francs, in addition to the contribution to the budget of the Association which each denomination had agreed to make. This offering was the very first income that Wycliffe Togo received for its operation.

This financial contribution from a local Togolese church for the support of the Bible translation movement let us catch a glimpse of the contribution in human and spiritual resources, as well as the use of future translations in the Church. For us, it was a huge prophetic sign. The support of the Church is the key to success. This support can be compared to the offering of the widow in the Temple in Jerusalem in front of our Lord Jesus Christ (Mark 12:41). She came with a generous heart, without being forced, and she was greatly praised by the Lord. Thereafter, the local Church would take the lead in supporting the realisation of Bible translation in Togo, and was proof that the translations into the mother tongue would be used, and that the receiving communities would be transformed.

Unfortunately, our naïvety meant that we did not quickly appreciate the deep impact that dependence on the support of western missions in Africa had had on the local Church. The glow of commitment that the Holy Spirit had aroused in the local Togolese Church dissipated very quickly with the complicity of those who looked askance at the birth of a Wycliffe mission in Togo and elsewhere in Africa. The strategy for stifling this glow was the confusion sown among the leading agents of the association concerning its strategy which appeared opposed to all support coming from outside, which was not true. In reality, it was about promoting the development of partnership internally first of all. The pioneers dreamt of seeing a local Church responsible for its mission, and capable of changing dependence into partnership. They hoped that this change would begin with the members of the administration of the Association, and after that influence the churches and institutions from which the members of the two component parts of the administration of Wycliffe Togo, the Board of Directors and the Executive Committee, before going outside Togo. As the wise Indian Gandhi said: "Become the change that you want to see in the world."

But as the saying goes, "What you are used to becomes second nature". We would have to wait for the change to take place. The charm of dependence on outside funding inhibited all the efforts of the steering committee to encourage the local Togolese church to support Wycliffe Togo in the realisation of translating the Bible in Togo. The programme of missionary weeks started by the local churches to support Wycliffe Togo in its mission for Bible translation and literacy was simply forgotten. The glow of mobilising resources from within the Togolese

Church for supporting the Bible translation movement slowly dissipated. 'The Mission of GOd' for the translation of the Bible was reduced to 'the sending of funding from outside' to realise translation projects and for the support of the movement.

In fact, 'the Mission of God'[4] is done through the Church, wherever it is, and it provides for the needs of its work, according to I Corinthians 9:7-12:

> Who serves as soldier at his own expense? Who plants a vineyard and does not eat its grapes? Who tends a flock and does not drink its milk? Do I say this merely on human authority? Doesn't the Law say the same thing? For it is written in the Law of Moses: *'Do not muzzle an ox while it is treading out the grain.'* Is it about oxen that God is concerned? Surely he says this for us, doesn't he? Yes, this was written for us, because whoever ploughs and threshes should be able to do so in the hope of sharing in the harvest. If we have sown spiritual seed among you, is it too much if we reap a material harvest from you? If others have this right of support from you, shouldn't we have it all the more? But we did not use this right. On the contrary, we put up with anything rather than hinder the gospel of Christ.

So, it is not excessive to ask the local African Church to support financially and materially the realisation of Bible translation and literacy in the mother tongues of Africa. After all, the African Church is there for African communities, and the African communities are there for the African Church.

---

[4]'The Mission of God' is the English translation of the Latin expression *'missio Dei'*. The expression was first used by the German missiologist Karl Hartenstein. For him, the only possible response to God's mission, as God's movement in history, is obedience by the Church.

Whom should we obey, God or man?

The birth of a Wycliffe mission in Togo had surprised many people. Until that time, Africa was considered a mission field reserved for SIL and not for Wycliffe. The West was considered the only source for the sending of missionary translators. To go against this line of thought was perceived as rebellion. So our action which had led to the creation of Wycliffe Togo was not appreciated by everyone. The Togo-Benin branch of SIL had taken a considerable risk in allowing the emergence of a Wycliffe mission in Togo. This movement had to be stopped at all costs, and the birth of a second Wycliffe organisation in Benin had to be prevented. The official policy was for the creation of a single structure for the Bible translation movement in the whole of Africa, called Wycliffe Africa. The leaders of the young organisation Wycliffe Togo began to be worried. The fears came from two sources: the threat that permission to use the name 'Wycliffe' for the Togolese organisation could be withdrawn, and the fact that the ex-president, David Cummings, was not an official delegate of Wycliffe International at the founding congress of Wycliffe Togo. Wycliffe Togo began to be spoken of as though it were a child that was not wanted.

Persuade at all costs

"Since, then, we know what it is to fear the Lord, we try to persuade others. What we are is plain to God, and I hope it is also plain to your conscience." (II Corinthians 5 :11).

Faced with opposition, we sought to persuade everyone who would listen to us. The promoters of Wycliffe Togo launched an operation of information to explain their vision. The letter we had written to the Executive Committee of SIL

Togo-Benin and to the conference of SIL in Africa in October 1992 about our vision was duplicated and distributed. A new communication was addressed to the first leaders of Wycliffe Africa and SIL. Our communication was as follows:

> To Dr. John Bendor-Samuel, Director, Wycliffe Africa
>
> From Napo Jérémie Poidi, Director, Wycliffe Togo
>
> CC: Dr. John Watters, Executive Director of Wycliffe International and SIL International; Rev. Dick Hugoniot, President of WBTI; Dr. Conrad Dogba, President of the Board of Directors of Wycliffe Togo; the members of the Executive Committee of Wycliffe Togo; the leaders of the Churches in Togo,
>
> Date: 7th March 2002
>
> Dear John,
>
> Among the important resolutions of the most recent Conferences of Wycliffe International and SIL International at Waxhaw (USA), there was the one which recognised that the translation of the Bible is the responsibility of the whole Church throughout the world. Nevertheless, this recognition is insufficient if the Church in the four corners of the earth does not take on board its responsibilities for the translation of the Bible.
>
> But how will the Church in Africa carry out its responsibilities if it does not have an appropriate understanding of the vision for Bible translation? How will the church in each African country understand if no one is sent to serve it? And how can anyone serve the local Church if a Wycliffe Association is not specifically set up in each country?

In April 2000, the outgoing president of Wycliffe International, David Cummings, came to Togo. He came to give an address to the founding congress which was going to establish the Wycliffe Togo Association. We believe that Wycliffe Togo was born at the right time, according to the will of God and for His glory. We praise the Lord for the recent decision of the Executive Director of Wycliffe and SIL International, Dr. John Watters, to grant accreditation to our Association. Very fortunately, at the same time, the Government of Togo granted official recognition to Wycliffe Togo as a non-profit organisation in Togo.

In the 14th century, John Wycliffe was the first person to effectively embrace the vision for translating the Bible into English, his mother-tongue. He translated the Bible into English from the existing Latin version, to the great benefit of the ordinary people.

In the same way, within the Organisation of Wycliffe and SIL International, we believe that the true well-being of mankind is found in understanding and obeying the Word of God, according to Psalm 1:2-3.

For us, a Wycliffe Association in Africa, like Wycliffe Togo, is like a tree planted beside a stream. This tree can be planted in every country without exception, not only in Africa, but also in Asia and in the Pacific, just as it has been planted in America and in Europe. The roots of the tree are the churches in the respective countries. The roots penetrate as far as the water-table underneath the ground. This water-table symbolises the Word of God. The trunk of the tree symbolises the ministry of Wycliffe Togo in the local churches, but it is also the tool of the Church to serve the ethnic and linguistic communities.

One of the effects of the ministry of a Wycliffe Association is its contribution to the unity of the Church in the country. Another effect is education, that is, the contribution of information which is useful to the Church to equip her for her service in the Mission of God. The impact will be the motivation and the effective involvement of the local church in God's work in general. In this way, the ministry of translating the Bible goes beyond the translation of the Book.

In the meantime, what place does SIL have in the country where it works? In reality, SIL is a branch of the 'Wycliffe tree'. It is the branch which represents research and translation in practice. The other branches of the 'Wycliffe tree' are found in the following domains: the resources in personnel, and those which are spiritual, financial and material. The ethnic and linguistic groups are represented by the leaves.

In nature, there are big trees and little trees. It is the same for the 'Wycliffe tree'. But what is important is that each tree should bear fruit, whether it is large or small.

The growth of the 'Wycliffe tree' in Togo depends on God alone. Our responsability is to plant it and to water it day and night, with our prayers and our programmes in the churches, but also with the other Wycliffe organisations in the West, with the NBTOs, SIL and other partners.

We want to thank you for your collaboration as brothers in Christ, your prayers and your support which you have given to our young Wycliffe Togo Association. We are grateful to Wycliffe USA, Wycliffe Switzerland, and to JAARS for the recent visit of their representatives to Togo.

'May the Lord bless WBTI and SIL International in their walk in love and unity for the translation of the Bible, with the collaboration of the local Church on the African continent.

Yours very respectfully,

Napo

A surprise visit

This communication went viral. On 2nd April 2003, the new President of Wycliffe International, Rev. Dick Hugoniot, arrived in Lome for a three-day visit, in order to see for himself what was happening within the Wycliffe Togo organisation. It was a great honour for the young Wycliffe Togo mission. During these three days, Rev. Hugoniot had a series of working meetings with church leaders, the Board of Directors chaired by Dr. Konrad Dogba, and with the Executive Committee of Wycliffe Togo in turn; the meetings were both fruitful and friendly. He was also taken to take part in the 2003 Easter conferences of certain churches, in particular the annual conference of the pastors and deacons of the Baptist Convention of Togo, which took place in Kpekpleme (Prefecture of the East-Mono) on the 3rd of April, and the meeting of the group of young intercessors for Wycliffe Togo. On the morning of the 4th of April, Rev. Hugoniot was able to take part in the Easter Conference of the Assemblies of God at Kpomegan (Prefecture of Hahotoé) and to visit the Anastasia Mercy Ship which had already been in Togolese waters for two months.

As a result of his visit to Togo and before his departure on 5th of April, Rev. Hugoniot, President of Wycliffe International, came to the conclusion that the vision and the birth of Wycliffe Togo was something that had come from God. As a result, he encouraged the leaders of the association to go forward, always keeping their eyes fixed on Jesus Christ, the good Shepherd. He then encouraged the local Church and the administration of Wycliffe Togo to make themselves wholly available to God for his mission.

So this was how Wycliffe International, by the word of its President, recognised Wycliffe Togo, and also encouraged the Togolese Church to take part in the realisation of Vision 2025. Many personal testimonies from the leaders of Churches, notably from Rev. Creppy Klozegbe, President of the Methodist Conference of Togo, from Rev. Milenovissi Akponou, President of the Church of Pentecost of Togo, from Rev. Gaston Kodjovi Anani, General Secretary of the Assemblies of God in Togo, and also from Dr. Konrad Dogba, President of the Board of Directors of Wycliffe Togo, convinced Rev. Hugoniot that what was happening in Togo was truly the work of God. Let us reflect on one of these testimonies:

> *My call to Wycliffe-Togo*[5]
>
> One afternoon in June 1984, I was at the Swiss consulate in London for the purpose of obtaining

[5] *The Translator – Languages at the Service of Development – News bulletin of the Wycliffe Togo Association*, no. 1, January 2004.

a visa for Switzerland where I was due to meet certain leaders of the World Health Organisation in Geneva. To my great surprise, there at the consulate I bumped into Napo Jérémie Poidi, an old student of mine, who, some years earlier, had taken my courses in animal biology at the University of Benin (now called the University of Lome). "What are you doing here, Mr. Poidi?" I asked him. This was his reply: "I have just finished my training in linguistics and I'm going to Geneva concerning the translation of the Bible into our mother tongues." "Why Bible translation?" I asked him. "The Lord has called me to the work of translating the Bible into my mother tongue," he said. His reply struck me like lightning, and both in the plane which took me from London to Geneva and in the one which took me from Geneva back to Accra, I couldn't stop thinking about this reply

Here are the thoughts which were going round in my head: here is a former student of mine to whom the Lord has spoken and given a special task... And you, who were this young man's teacher, what are you doing? Or don't you want to do anything for the Lord? But, as the popular saying goes: 'It is better late than never.' So it was in 1996, twelve years after that meeting, that Mr. Poidi came to me in my office in Lome to ask me if I would like to be part of a steering committee, the object of which was to see how they could help the translation of the Bible into the languages of Togo. I accepted this invitation, and became part of the group which met once a week in the home of Mr. Michel Dagoh, who at the time was General

Secretary to the Minister of Foreign Affairs and Cooperation. During our meetings, we prayed and watched films about Bible translation.

Appetite comes while you are eating, they say. These meetings gave me the taste and the burning desire to belong to a group for the translation of the Bible. As I read Christian literature, the light of translating the Bible dawned on me more and more. Why translate the Bible?

The Bible, the Word of God, is a light (Psalm 119). It alone can meet the spiritual needs of every man, woman and child. It alone can show the way of salvation and how to grow in Jesus Christ. But before the Word of God can bring light into people's lives, they must be able to read it in the language of their heart, the one they understand best. In the regions where the Bible has not been translated into the local languages, the inhabitants think that God doesn't speak their language. That is why for me, everyone has the right to read the Bible in his own language. No people-group can be considered reached with the Gospel while the Scriptures have not been translated into their language. They constitute the foundation for establishing a viable Christian community, capable of thinking and living as a result. A Peruvian lady, when she heard the Bible read in a language related to her own, exclaimed one day: "Is there someone who can learn my language and give us messages which we can understand easily?" Without the Bible in her mother tongue, she could not understand the Bible stories which she heard from someone else. God can use the translation of the Bible to draw this woman, and other people like her, to himself. So I support this vision which wants every people-group to have access to the Bible in their heart-language, the language which they understand best.

> Dr. Konrad Dogba,
> President of the Board of
> Directors of Wycliffe Togo

With these vibrant testimonies and the concrete results produced by the Bible translation movement in Togo, the young Wycliffe Togo Association took root little by little. It was officially recognised by the Togolese state in 2002 and accepted as a member of the great family of the Wycliffe Global Alliance.

The appeal made by John Agamah to Wycliffe in England in the 1950s for the translation of the Bible into African languages was in effect a double appeal. Uncle Agamah was also addressing the local African Church, inviting her to take part in the 'Mission of God' in every ethnic and linguistic group in Africa, by supporting the translation of the Bible into the mother tongues with all of her strength.

In Togo, the appeal by Uncle John Agamah was heard and responded to. It is true that the beginning was small, but God gave it success. Tribute should be paid to the local Togolese Church for all its efforts and commitment for the translation of the Bible into the mother tongues of Togo and beyond. In ten years, the local Church, through its 'arm' Wycliffe-Togo, has come a considerable distance by pioneering certain activities, notably by:

1. Awakening the conscience of the people of God in Togo about the necessity of listening to the Word of God in our mother tongues.

2. Promoting the development of partnerships with the churches and other institutions for the purpose of Bible translation and literacy in the Church in Togo.

3. Mobilising resources, human, material, financial and spiritual for the purpose of accomplishing the task on the field.

The results are in proportion to the engagement of the local Church, in the following domains:

1. The collaboration established within the Church in its entirety, and with certain ministries and partners in particular.

2. The sending of about 20 missionaries into the field of linguistic research, translation, literacy, intercessory prayer, and Scripture engagement in the mother tongues of Togo.

3. Partial support for the missionaries has been assured by the churches, and there have been substantial financial contributions from these churches to the budget of the movement for translation in Togo.

4. Prayer and intercession have been mobilised in the Church for the Mission of God, for Bible translation and literacy.

5. Pastoral and moral support has been obtained from church leaders.

6. Collaboration between local associations for the translation of the Bible have been initiated on the field in Togo.

However, this raft of successes must not mask our weaknesses, in particular the very weak mobilization of resources for meeting the needs of the ministry of Bible translation and a strong dependence on external financial support, and the absolute necessity of maintaining a fervent love for each other so that we can build a community for Christ. Martin Luther King[6] said: "We need to learn to love each other like brothers or get ready to die like imbeciles." In this regard we recognize the weak beginnings of the movement. Nevertheless, we do not in any way despise them. This is because we can always count on the mercy of God and his faithfulness to the promises he has made to us, he who has established an eternal Covenant with us in his Son our Lord. On this rests our whole salvation!

> "No, in all these things we are more than conquerors through him who loved us. For I am convinced that neither death nor life, neither angels nor demons, neither the present nor the future, nor any powers, neither height nor depth, nor anything else in all creation, will be able to separate us from the love of God that is in Christ Jesus our Lord." (Romans 8:37-39)

---

[6] In a sermon preached on 31st of March 1968 at the National Episcopal Cathedral in Washington.

Chapter 6

The Bible translation movement today and tomorrow

The goal of the Bible translation movement in Togo is to have a positive impact on the lives of her people. To achieve this, the mission Wycliffe-Togo is doing everything possible so that the Holy Scriptures can be accessible to all those who do not yet have them in their own language. We do this by:

1. "Using all possible means to make the Word of God (source of salvation by faith in Jesus Christ) available to each ethnic and linguistic group in their mother tongue."

2. Serving the Church by raising awareness about the Mission of God (Missio Dei).

3. Encouraging understanding of the value of the mother tongue and its wider use in all aspects of life.

4. Mobilising resources and building capacity so that the Scriptures translated into these languages will be well used.

5. Bringing literacy to the communities.

As every tree draws sap from its roots, in the same way the movement draws its strength from the Church, the Body of Christ in the whole country, and from every person or institution which is willing to be involved. In order to achieve this, appropriate partnerships need to be developed with the Church on the one hand, and with ministries, local translation associations, foreign missions, governmental and non-governmental associations on the other. In this way the Bible translation movement will be able to mobilise all available means for linguistic research, Bible translation, literacy, Scripture engagement and the use of languages for the development of the people.

But above all, it is the local Church which is responsible for putting into motion the translation of the Bible in Togo and beyond. This is because the local Church is of supreme worth, and the foundation on which the translation of the Bible rests in actual fact. The strength of any building is in its foundation. The Bible translation movement mobilises, recruits, and sends the people who are called from within the Church for the work of Bible translation in Togo and outside of Togo.

The importance of literacy

However, what we really want to see is not only a translation of the Bible in our mother tongues, but the Holy Scriptures being used, and that this should lead to salvation by faith in Jesus Christ, and to the transformation and development of those who believe. The greatest obstacle to this is the intellectual and educational development necessary to overcome illiteracy. If the language of certain people-groups has never been written, no one can read or write it. This is why the members sent to the field as translators begin by breaking the barrier of illiteracy, by learning the language and the culture, analysing the sound system and the grammar of the language to help the people develop a written form of the their mother tongue, with its own alphabet, grammar, dictionary and all the other things which come with a written language. Once the mother tongue is in written form, translation can begin. Mother-tongue translators need to be trained, begin working and receive ongoing professional development. At the same time, a literacy programme must be developed, so that the population can learn to read and write in their mother tongue. This is how linguistic research can lead to a written mother tongue, which opens the way for literacy and Bible translation, and to spiritual development according to how people use the translated Holy Scriptures in their everyday lives.

But people need more than spiritual development. The people and the authorities which govern them are conscious of the need to improve agricultural techniques for a more effective production of food. They also need better medical facilities, and a greater knowledge of hygiene to improve their health.

Furthermore, the population will come to realise their need of a political system which is more democratic, for more social justice and for education. For this too, there are government ministries and other organisations which specialise in these domains. Collaboration between all these agencies is what is necessary to enable people to move from oral communication only to written communication in their mother tongues.

Illiteracy is a barrier to all the benefits brought by all these partners in development mentioned above. Their efforts in development suffer from the fact that the people in the villages cannot read a brochure or take notes during training workshops, nor keep accounts or even write their names. Oral communication alone does not allow for the whole message to be communicated or retained for any length of time. In every situation where the written form of the language of a people-group, and material to teach reading and writing has been developed, it becomes possible for all these other organisations to use the written mother tongue to encourage development in all the domains of the life of its people group. It is only in an environment where the written mother tongue is used in all aspects of life, and where people have learnt to use it to express all aspects of their culture, that the translated Holy Scriptures will be used effectively, certainly by future generations. This is a summary of the challenge we face! All possible and available resources must be mobilised and channelled into a legal entity like Wycliffe Togo. The Association will be a mission of linguistic development, an 'arm' of the Church in Togo, which works for the promotion of Bible translation, literacy, engagement with the Holy Scriptures, and the revitalisation of Togolese mother tongues by their development and use.

Beyond Vision 2025

The Bible translation movement is charting a course across Africa and the rest of the world, through numerous partners committed to working together for the realisation of a common vision. This vision, Vision 2025, was adopted in 1999 by the great family of organisations called the Wycliffe Global Alliance and SIL International. Each national Wycliffe organisation, such as Wycliffe Togo, is autonomous and brings its particular contribution to the great family of the Wycliffe Global Alliance.

For us, we must go further than Vision 2025. It is not enough to complete the mission of translating the Bible, but above all the final product must be valued and be the means of transforming the people for whom it was translated. In addition to the promotion of the Holy Scriptures in the mother tongues, no effort should be spared to facilitate the development of the ordinary church members, and the whole community, by promoting a biblically-based education for all. This should begin by teaching children the Gospel in their mother tongue when they first go to school. The mother tongue is the heart-language of the child, or indeed of the soul of the people who speak it. The ultimate aim is to educate each child so that he can understand the meaning of his life from a young age.

As the Scripture says: "What good will it be for someone to gain the whole world, yet forfeit their soul ?" (Matthew 16 :26) In the same way it is of no benefit to African people to master a foreign language, be it European or African, if it means they lose their own heart language, which is their 'soul'. The promotion of a people's mother tongue is therefore the means of salvation for the people in question, because the Word of God translated into that language can penetrate more deeply into the hearts of the people and promote their complete transformation.

Going beyond Vision 2025, the local Church must take responsibility for the future revision of current translations of the Bible, and for the production of those new translations, and the publication and dissemination of the Holy Scriptures in local languages, in order to provide for the needs of future generations.

Such initiatives and many others will enable a solid foundation to be laid for the development of African thinking in general, and in particular Christian thinking.

However, there are numerous hindrances which can be an obstacle to the anticipated normal development of the translation movement. Among these hindrances which are already visible are:

1. The domination by foreign, Western languages and cultures.

2. The local African Church has turned in on itself rather than towards the communities to which it is called to bring the grace of the Lord. Jesus said: "My prayer is not that you take them out of the world but that you protect them from the evil one." (John 17 :15)

3. Africans themselves neglect the enormous potential of their people for their own development, and for that of the rest of the world.

4. The African elite undervalues African languages, culture and values which are an essential element in the search for development in African countries. They hide behind the great number of languages in a country, and the small number of the speakers of these languages.

5. The high level of illiteracy in each language group.

6. The high number of illiterate people in the churches, who cannot read or write in any language, including their own mother tongue.

7. The lack of appropriate didactic material in the mother tongues already written.

8. The insufficient number of literacy teachers and promoters of the Scriptures to meet the needs of each linguistic group.

9. In particular, there is a lack of common strategy, a Marshall plan for all the agencies operating in a country, to promote literacy and the reading of Scriptures in the mother tongues, and the promotion of their cultures.

10. The lack of initiative for the overall development and use of the mother tongues spoken in each country. The object of such an initiative would be: training for the trainers in the mother tongues, and training for the translators of such documents as the Constitution of the country, the Rights of Man and the Rights of Children. The literature and cultural values of the peoples, and all literature for education, both Christian and secular, should be produced in the mother tongues, at competitive prices. Such an initiative would open an opportunity for employment, the exchange of experiences and evaluation in the domain of education in the mother tongues.

Such an operation, taking up the challenge for all the peoples, languages and cultures of our countries is not impossible, far from it. In Togo, for example, the partners in the development of our languages, one of which is the governmental department in charge of literacy, are among the most precious resources to achieve this. We should also certainly make an inventory of other potential partners who have a common interest with us for the development and use of the Togolese mother tongues, and motivate them.

Like a river, the movement will grow larger all the time, being enriched at every stage by the inspiration and contribution of partners with many and various talents, like tributaries which flow into a river. These partners do for the Bible translation movement what tributaries do for a river. In this way, they enrich the enterprise and as a result constitute the principal means of overcoming the obstacles which have been mentioned previously.

Nevertheless, in Togo the opportunities for success are there, as is shown by the results attained in the country over the years :

1. The local language associations at work in the different languages : ACEB (Bassar), APSEK (Kabiye), ATAPEB (Moba), ACPLL (Lama), ASDN (Nawdm), ATADEC (Gangam), ACATBLI (Ife), PATBID (Ikposso), OADI (Igo), ABTem (Tem), APLA (Akebou), etc.

2. The work of researchers of all kinds who work tirelessly in fundamental and applied linguistics on the languages of Togo.

3. The teams for the translation of the Holy Scriptures in many of these languages in Togo.

4. Translations of the Bible, or portions of the Bible, are available in many languages.

5. A rich and varied literature is available in the mother tongues.

6. Literacy workers are active in the local languages.

7. There are workers who promote the use of the Holy Scriptures actively engaged on the field.

8. There are local churches motivated to support the work if they understand the vision.

9. The efforts made by numerous NGOs.

10. The Universities in Lome and Kara are training young linguists.

In addition to these, we can add the partners who are deeply involved in the development of our languages, in translation and in literacy: the societies for the development of the local languages, and the Cultural Centres.

One question remains, however: How can we arrive at this synergy and answer the call of people-groups who are still in need ? We suggest some avenues towards a solution:

1. Put the emphasis on literacy, and on reading and engaging with the Holy Scriptures in the the mother tongue in every church and ethnic community in the country.

2. Promote the mother tongues by nationwide programmes such as the 'Month of the Mother Tongue'. Each community or local church is invited to consecrate a Sunday of its choice to hold their services in the mother tongues represented among them, by having prayers, Bible readings, worship and dancing in each of those mother tongues, and by wearing traditional costumes, for the glory of God. This event will be considered as a cultural day, set aside for the promotion of the mother tongue of the ethnic group concerned. The whole population will be involved, including the local authorities, both administrative and traditional. World Literacy Day, 8th September, would be a suitable day for this celebration.

3. Organise a 'Mother Tongue Fair', an activity which offers an opportunity for discovering the treasures which are contained in our mother tongues for our history, customs, beliefs, technologies and cultures; a plea for the development and use of our mother tongues, and a meeting between the promoters of the Scriptures and writers in our mother tongues, and an opportunity to promote books in the mother tongues by holding exhibitions and showing how they impact humanity.

4. Organise Inspirational Days for each local language to promote its use, its translation, literacy, Scripture promotion, and then to mobilise resources for the work in the language in question, in each prefecture where the people has its origin, during the annual traditional festivals.

National campaigns for reading and writing in the mother tongue

The most effective solution would be to develop a common strategy encompassing all those involved in the field of literacy for launching periodic large national campaigns across the whole country to promote reading in the mother tongue. In the new context of globalisation, searching for ways and means of development in African nations cannot continue to ignore the irreplaceable role of the mother tongues spoken by the people. International exchange is no longer limited to the domains of politics and economics, but also includes cultural, moral and spiritual values, and for these the mother tongues are the effective means of transmission.

History is full of examples of modern nations who have made good use of their mother tongues in the search for development. The examples of Japan and South Korea are an inspiration for us. A report from the United Nations Programme for Development in 2008 reveals that the level of literacy in Japan had reached 99%, and that of South Korea 93.5%. But before these two nations reached this level, they had both been through a period of social and economic decline and a deterioration in their educational systems after the Second World War.

Because of poverty, the number of literate people in South Korea was only 20% of the population, which means that 80% were illiterate.

In Japan, the school curriculum was considered a failure because of the high number of cases of aggression and of dropping out of school because of overwork. Sixty-five years later, Japan and Korea have shown that it is possible to promote the development of a nation by applying strategies which increase the level of literacy in the population. These strategies are, among others, a clear policy led by the government for the promotion of reading. It is achieved by:

a) creating libraries in every part of the country

b) campaigns to encourage the population to read and to use these libraries.

c) making child care workers aware of the need to encourage the children under their care to read in their mother tongue, and by mobilising the information technology necessary to encourage the development of reading.

d) collaboration with the NGOs and with local authorities to promote reading.

e) creating teaching materials to encourage the analysis of the content of what is read.

In South Korea, in the 1970s, around 35,000 little libraries were built in villages throughout Korea. Every Korean family encouraged reading in their household. There was a little family library in each house, containing works about the values, culture and history of the people which stimulated national pride, and encyclopedias were created which enabled children to get to know the history of the surrounding countries.

The tangible result of these efforts was the development which these two countries, Japan and South Korea, experienced thanks to education and the increase of knowledge among the population by the promotion of reading in the mother tongue.

The contribution which Wycliffe Togo and its partners can make to such national literacy campaigns and for reading in the local languages would be to organise seminars across the country for training the trainers in the techniques of literacy teaching, promoting the Scriptures, and encouraging authors to write in their languages for their communities. Those who have been trained will have as their mission to create new literacy classes and reading groups for their communities. Collaboration with governments and other partners, the churches, and the NGOs who are operating in different localities will enable the campaigns to be repeated from time to time and in this way encourage reading and writing to become embedded in the life of the populations who will benefit from them.

When the passage from orality to writing has been achieved, the populations who have benefited will have the means of participating actively in the development of their community and their nation. They will see the interest that the authorities of their nation have shown in their languages, and thus in their identity and dignity. "Primary education for all" will no longer be an empty phrase. The moral, spiritual and cultural values will find their place again among our populations thanks to the renewal of our mother tongues and our cultures, but particularly thanks to the translation of the Testament of God and literature edifying for the people. The national reconciliation so sought after on the continent will become a reality.

Moving from oral to written communication for lasting development in African nations

Is it necessary to write our African languages, when we consider how many there are compared with the small number of their speakers—hundreds or tens of thousands of people? What profit will be gained, by these ethnic communities, by the nation and by the Church?

The mother tongue, as we have described it above, is the basic cultural tool of each human community, a means of communication, exchange and at the same time an instrument for mastering scientific knowledge and technology which is indispensable to the progress and all-round development of the people of all nations and races. The mother tongue is therefore a treasure, as we have said, for our history, our customs, our traditional skills, our cultures and our beliefs. The mother tongue is the 'soul' of the people who speak it.

No society can change unless it breaks with its traditional way of life and aspires to a future which is much better and presses forwards towards it. The progress from oral to written communication in western societies proves this. The necessity of written language has become so obvious that it is no longer questioned. But experience today shows that a simple transcription of oral communication is not sufficient to produce this necessary break which leads from traditional oral civilisation to modern written civilisation.

We need to ask ourselves the following question: if we who have orality as our heritage, should we not just profit from this expertise ? In other words, instead of seeking to move from orality to written communication, would it not be more useful to *develop* orality by making use of the new audio-visual technologies in communication to take advantage of new knowledge, and so benefit our peoples?

Can we completely set aside the writing of our languages in this quest for development? Do we believe that people really need to have their language written?

These are some of many questions which need to be explored. As we reflect on them, let us consider four critical needs for which the writing of our languages remains a priority in spite of everything:

1. The need to communicate with people separated by distance and time.

   How would the message of the Bible have come down to us if God had not ordered that it should be written? How would the order given by our Lord Jesus Christ to his Church have been carried out without the message of the gospel being written and transmitted to those who live far away? When the transmitter is physically absent, the written message, following the rules of the orthography of the language, can easily be transmitted to those who are absent, or far away, or kept for future generations. In this way, the new knowledge is preserved and transmitted to a wider and more varied audience.

2. The need to affirm the identity of each people group and its mother-tongue as an appropriate instrument for communication:

   > "Undoubtedly there are all sorts of languages in the world, yet none of them is without meaning." (I Corinthians 14:10)

   To write a language is to show that it has the means of communication like other languages, and is thus able to express modern ideas. If a language is written, the speakers can use it in their everyday lives as an instrument for mastering the principles which improve the well-being of its speakers.

3. The need to preserve the cultural, economic and political heritage of each people-group in relation to others on the national scale.

   Every ethnic community has a certain cultural, economic and political capital which can only be established in relation to other peoples when their language is written and has complete autonomy. African peoples are unfortunately in a state of economic and political dependence, because they need French, English, Portuguese or Spanish for their contacts with the outside world; this is particularly the case when it comes to the education of their children. When they choose education manuals in French or English, Africans are dependant on the French or the English. As a result, African mother tongues are dominated by these two written languages, which provide them with all their written knowledge.

   To move from oral to written communication certainly necessitates the creation of a simple and consistent orthography, but it also requires the creation of favourable conditions for a transition from orality to writing within the linguistic communities. The benefit to be obtained from it can be summarised in these terms: the greater well-being of the communities, and the accomplishment of the Mission of God and of our Lord Jesus Christ who calls his disciples to make people of every nation his disciples.

There is therefore a challenge to be taken up for every language, and this challenge is threefold: first of all, the challenge of the development and use of the mother tongue; then that of literacy and of producing audio-visual materials; and lastly that of translating written knowledge into the mother tongue. The aim is to make the language an instrument of cultural development and the mastery of knowledge and power.

4. The need to relearn our African mother tongues.

According to the missiologist Kwame Bediako[1], those who have most need of their mother tongues are African intellectuals.

Even though it is not obvious to a large number of people, this need is none the less real. The increased ignorance of the mother tongues and of African culture among the intellectuals of Africa is both a challenge and an opportunity for writing and the promotion of written literature, and at the same time the production of audio-visual material in our African languages.

To take up this challenge, we must develop partnerships with the local political and administrative authorities, and

---

[1] Kwame Bédiako (2004b). "The Relevance of Bible Translation For Church Growth". In: *FOBAC*. Accra, Ghana: Christialler Institute of Theology, Mission and Culture

then with all those who use the mother tongues. There is therefore a need for raising awareness and sharing the vision with the educated people of each people-group.

Concerted action must be taken to work together for a common goal to which each partner will bring its particular contribution.

What kind of development for our African nations?

What does the development of a nation mean ? It is a difficult question to answer. Our vision for the development of a nation is inspired by the vision given by C.E. Black[2] in his article 'Dynamics of Modernisation', in particular in the chapter about the meaning of development. The author criticises the fact that it is usually only the economic aspect of a nation which is taken into account for measuring its level of development. The development of a nation should be measured in relation to the whole potential of human beings and their social integration into the heart of their nation. Here is the crux of the matter: many African intellectuals have difficulty integrating into the heart of their ethnic and linguistic communities, simply because of their ignorance of their own mother tongue and culture.

The conditions which must be fulfilled to reach this level of human development include economic factors such as satisfying the need for food and clothes, and for work and equal shares in wealth; but it is also necessary to satisfy the need for a good education, for freedom of speech, and for political and economic freedom within the nation. Black has also indicated the five domains of development which are interconnected:

[2] C E Black (1966). *Dynamics of Modernisation*. Harper & Row.

the intellectual, political, economic, social and psychological aspects of life.

After studying the history of the development of the modern world, he draws attention to the fact that the process of the development of nations is both creative and destructive. In this way, we can see that the states which have the greatest modernisation are those which at the same time have the greatest capacity to destroy humanity and its environment. However, in spite of the creative and destructive elements of development, every nation prefers to come out of underdevelopment rather than to stay in it.

Among the most important aspects to be considered in the process of development for Africa are the economic, politico-judicial, sociocultural, intellectual and educational aspects. The question to be decided is whether the mother tongues are a key factor in the development of these important aspects. What are the factors which inhibit the development of the whole potential of the human being, for example from the point of view of economics? Do our mother tongues have a part to play?

In 1954, the United Nations made a list of twelve domains[3] which are important for successful social development. These are health, nutrition, education, literary abilities, conditions of work, unemployment, consumption and saving, transport, lodging, clothes, leisure activities, social security, and human liberty. These aspects are also considered indicators of economic development.

So we return to our question: does the mother-tongue have a role to play in facilitating or restricting the potential of human beings to participate in the economic and social

[3]United Nations, *Survey of Social Statistics*, 17th December, 1954.

development of their people-group or of their nation? We would say, Yes, our mother tongues have a very important role to play.

What about the political and judicial development of our nations? What role do our mother tongues have in these domains? The external aspect of this political and judicial domain refers to the security of our national frontiers and maintaining good relations with neighbouring countries. Internally, the principal aspects of the domain are the elaboration and adoption of a constitution acceptable to all within the nation, the selection of a leadership which will be duly and legally elected, law-making and the enforcement of justice in the nation. The development of this political and judicial domain implies that the majority, if not all, of the population of a country should actively participate in the relevant activities. To achieve this, the constitution should be translated and made accessible to everyone in the language they understand best. Taking part in elections should be done freely, and reflect the opinion of the citizens regarding the political life of their nation. The ruling class should be able to communicate regularly with the population in all its aspects about the way they are managing the affairs of state, and the laws which have been voted should be communicated to everyone in a language with which they are familiar.

Communicating with all the population in our multilingual nations is naturally a major problem. How can we facilitate this communication with everyone in the language they understand best, let alone respect the right of each citizen to have this communication in writing in his own language? The 'African Cultural Charter' adopted in 1976 at the Summit of Heads of State gathered at Port-Louis (Mauritius), and the 'Plan for the Development of Africa' also adopted by the heads of State meeting in Lagos (Nigeria) in 1980, recommended that priority be given to 'the transcription, teaching, and development of the use of national languages in such a way that they become languages used for broadcasting and the development of science and technology.' They also encouraged 'the introduction and intensification of the teaching of national languages in order to accelerate the process of economic, social, political and cultural development of our states.' Our unwritten languages constitute a hindrance to this. Our linguists must therefore make a contribution towards facilitating the political and judicial development of our nations.

Another domain is that of promoting cultural diversity. Many people, including our governments, support this idea and are even willing to struggle to promote it. Professor Gilbert Ansre[4] recommends that an inclusive linguistic policy is the best choice for African countries in the construction of their respective nations. When nationalism takes into account the integration of all the linguistic and ethnic groups of which the nation-state is composed, it is easier to achieve a nation which is culturally integrated. But when nationalism to create a nation-state becomes selective, the cultural integration of all the ethnic and linguistic groups in the country becomes difficult and a source of tension within that nation. As the African Cultural Charter states: "The affirmation of a national identity must not be made at the expense of the impoverishment and subjection of the diverse cultures which exist in the same country."

For our growing African nations, the 'golden rule'[5] should be applied concerning our peoples and their languages. Respect for diversity is a condition for the harmonious develop-

---

[4]Gilbert Ansre (1990). *National Development and Language: A Prologue to Language Policy Formulation and Implementation*.

[5]"So in everything, do to others what you would have them do to you, for this sums up the Law and the Prophets." (Matthew 7:12)

ment of a nation. The following examples reinforce this analysis. Take the case of France, where the provincial dialects were marginalised in favour of the dialect of the Île-de-France (that is, of the Paris area). Fortunately, we are now witnessing the re-emergence of these dialects and cultures, such as Breton and Alsatian. Another case is in Spain with the Catalan language. For a long time, the teaching of Catalan was forbidden in the school curricula. Since Catalonia is the richest province of the country, it is seeking to separate from Spain, in spite of opposition from the rest of the country. In Catalonia today, the Catalan language has been reintroduced and children are again learning Catalan at school. A translation of the Bible in Catalan has existed for several centuries side-by-side with Spanish. We could also cite the case of the Gaelic languages in Wales and in Scotland, where English dominates.

What is most important for our African nations is to reach the point where the gap between the elite and the masses within a nation is minimised, if not totally reduced to zero. The cultural and artistic characteristics of each ethnic and linguistic group should be appreciated and treated equally, and promoted without discrimination. The promotion of cultural and artistic diversity means the promotion of the linguistic, cultural and artistic values of all the ethnic groups within a country. This promotion necessarily involves the development of the languages spoken by these people-groups.

Intellectual and educational development is fundamental for any country seeking its development as a nation. Intellectual development means the increase of understanding, the control of self and its environment, the accumulation of knowledge, and the methods of explaining and applying it to resolve the needs of human beings and eventually of all of creation, and the development and dissemination of new ideas.

It is recognised that intellectual development is the driving force of of all development within a nation.

But intellectual development has to be transmitted from one generation to another. It is the transmission of the intellectual development acquired by a community to other members of the same community which we call education. To educate a human being consists of preparing that person to participate fully in the development of their society. How the individual understands all of their environment, spiritual, physical, social and psychological, and the possession of all the necessary technology, are the signs and precursors of a real intellectual, educational and spiritual development.

So education becomes the most important means for achieving the liberty and prosperity to which a human being, a people-group or a nation aspires. Our unwritten languages are a real hindrance to the intellectual, educational and spiritual development of the local Church and of growing African nations.

According to Nelson Mandela, "education is the most powerful instrument that one can use to change the world." In the thinking of Mandela, education in the sense of transmitting the knowledge acquired by a community is a powerful instrument for change when this transmission is made in a person's mother tongue. That is what he meant when he said: "When you speak to someone in a language that he understands, it goes into his head. When you speak to him in his mother tongue, it goes into his heart."

Chapter 7

Epilogue

Towards a people who are free and prosperous

Round a table carefully laid in the middle of the living room of their house, Mr. Jonathan Weiss, my Professor of Hebrew at the Hebrew University of Jerusalem and the head of the family, was seated in the place of honour. To his right was his wife, then his two daughters, then his son, his son-in-law, and seven visitors, two women and five men, of whom I was one. In front of each seat was a card with the name of each guest written on it, and also the book of Haggadah, the book containing the rituals associated with the Jewish Passover. When 9pm struck, the night of celebration of the 'Seder' began. The 'Seder' means the commemoration of the 'Freedom of God' given to the people of Israel, when God brought them out of Egypt, the country of the Pharaohs. 'Then Moses said to the people, "Commemorate this day, the day you came out of Egypt, out of the land of slavery, because the Lord brought you out of it with a mighty hand. Eat nothing containing yeast.'" (Exodus 13:3)

Mr. Weiss made a brief introduction to the evening. Then began the traditional reading of the account of the escape from Egypt from the book of Haggadah. First of all it was the son-in-law who began the reading in Hebrew. Throughout the night, the reading was done in turn by all the guests around the table, in the language of each one: Hebrew, English, and French. The atmosphere was very peaceful, and we all had a feeling of communion and brotherhood. One of Mr. Weiss's daughters, Deborah, spoke from time to time in perfect English to explain the celebration as it proceeded. But it was the commentary by Mr. Weiss in particular which commanded our attention. It was inspired and full of wisdom. Here are some choice portions taken from this book.

What is freedom? What is it for?

The Seder, as we have said, is the commemoration of the freedom which God gave to the people of Israel when he brought them out of Egypt. But what is freedom? The deliverance from slavery in Egypt. In fact, it was synonymous with the birth of the nation, the nation of Israel. But the freedom of a nation cannot be obtained except on condition that each individual desires and actively seeks to be free. In this way there is a correlation between national and individual freedom. The two go together, and you cannot have one without the other. No Jew can seek his own freedom apart from the freedom of the nation of Israel. To put it another way, the body is dependant on its members and the members on the body in order to live.

This analysis shows clearly the similarity between Jewish and African thought: "I am because we are." The freedom and prosperity of the Church, just like that of Israel and that of our African nations cannot be realised except on condition that each Christian, each citizen or individual, no matter what his background, desires and searches for the freedom that Jesus Christ gives. "If the Son sets you free, you will be free indeed." (John 8 :36)

Can Israel enjoy fully the freedom it has obtained outside of Egypt? The answer to this question is 'No'!

Each of us dipped a finger into our glass of wine, and we all let a drop of wine fall on to our respective plates. On the instructions of the head of the family, we all repeated this action three times in succession. This action symbolises that the freedom of Israel was obtained at a price. This price was the suffering inflicted on the enemy, Egypt, which had held the Hebrews in slavery for four hundred years. Egypt had suffered at least ten plagues sent by God on the country for the freedom of the Hebrews.

This reality made Israel a nation which was unique in its kind and its values. While all people rejoice that their enemies have received the punishment they deserve, the Jewish people remind us that no one can really rejoice totally when their freedom results in the suffering of their enemies.

The price for the freedom of all people on earth has been paid by Jesus Christ. We also cannot truly rejoice in the freedom we have acquired in Jesus Christ until all people have access to the Word which leads to that freedom. The Bible says: "Love does not delight in evil but rejoices with the truth" (I Corinthians 13:6), because "Your word is truth" (John 17:17b). God has given us a Testament for an eternal inheritance of freedom in his Son. It is the Good News which will be the subject of great joy among all the peoples of the world. "But the angel said to them, 'Do not be afraid. I bring you good news of great joy that will be for all the people'." (Luke 2:10) The great challenge facing the Church today is to translate the Testament of God into all the languages for all the peoples and to do everything possible so that it should be read, believed and disseminated.

Let us always be grateful to God

The ritual of remembrance for the deliverance from Egypt (Haggadah) is the 'breath' by which Israel, the nation and the individual, breathes. Now, each breath we take reminds us of the grace of God in our lives. In the same way that the body has a continual need for breath in order to live, so the nation and each Israeli citizen needs to repeat the commemoration of the deliverance from Egypt, from generation to generation according to the command of the Lord, to remember what God did for their fathers. This life is the way of freedom which leads to God.

In the same way, God gives today a 'new breath', not only to Israel but also to all nations, tribes and languages, by his Son Jesus Christ who died on the cross at Golgotha. By this act, God delivers each human being from the slavery of sin, so that he can enter by grace and by faith in Jesus Christ into possession of an eternal inheritance. So let us always be grateful to God.

But what has happened to the promise God made to Abraham when he said : "I will make you into a great nation"?

After Abraham had received this promise from God, famine caused him to go down into Egypt. Later, the descendants of

Abraham also went down into Egypt. It was there that they multiplied even under the conditions of slavery. In the modern world, around 6 million Jews died in the Shoa (the Jewish Holocaust). Today, Jews represent a very small proportion of the world's population. There are about 14 million Jews in the world, of whom 6 million live in modern Israel, founded on 14th May 1948.

Where then is the promise God made to Abraham? Has it been fulfilled, or is it still to be fulfilled ? In every situation, we know that God is faithful. He has fulfilled his promises to Abraham. He will certainly fulfil them for everyone who trusts in him. Between Israel and the Church, there is continuity, not a replacement. "For God's gifts and his call are irrevocable." (Romans 11:29)

The symbolism of the commemoration of the deliverance from Egypt

The Bible teaches us that the Fathers of Israel suffered in Egypt (Genesis), and outside of Egypt (Exodus 12). On their way to the Promised Land, they suffered the bitterness and the barrenness of the desert. At the same time they also experienced the goodness of the Lord all along the way. May the descendants of Israel never forget the goodness of God towards them! They should always sing this chorus : "*Dai Enu, Dai Enu*" 'We will never forget him.'.

The Seder and the Haggadah were instituted to remind Israel and her descendants, from generation to generation, of the goodness of God. They give the opportunity to Israel to experience the joys and the sufferings that their ancestors experienced in their march towards the freedom and prosperity

EPILOGUE

which God promised them. The Seder begins with the suffering and ends with songs of praise and happiness to the living God for his grace towards Israel.

The quest for freedom and prosperity to which the peoples of the world so much aspire is satisfied in the Testament of God which the Testator, Jesus Christ, left us after his death on the cross of Calvary for our sins and to remove the curse from us. He said:

> "All authority in heaven and on earth has been given to me. Therefore go and make disciples of all nations, baptising them in the name of the Father and of the Son and of the Holy Spirit, teaching them to obey everything I have commanded you. And surely I am with you always, to the very end of the age." (Matthew 28 :18-20)

Let us arise in his name to translate and publish the Testament of God, that is, the Bible, into the languages of the world which still need it!

Bibliography

Abbott, Mary and Monica Cox (1966). *Collected field reports on the phonology of Basari*. Collected Language Notes 5. Legon: Institute of African Studies, University of Ghana.

Ansre, Gilbert (1990). *National Development and Language: A Prologue to Language Policy Formulation and Implementation*.

Bédiako, Kwame (2004a). *Jesus and the Gospel in Africa: History and Experience*. Maryknoll, NY: Orbis Books.

— (2004b). "The Relevance of Bible Translation For Church Growth". In: *FOBAC*. Accra, Ghana: Christialler Institute of Theology, Mission and Culture.

Bessong Aroga, P. D. (2006). *Bible et Transformation: l'exemple de Joseph, une inspiration pour l'intercession*. Yaoundé: Editions ADG.

Black, C E (1966). *Dynamics of Modernisation*. Harper & Row.

Bridge, Donald (1987). *Power Evangelism and The Word of God*. Eastbourne: Kingsway Publications.

Carson, A. D., ed. (2001). *New Testament Commentary Survey*. 5th edition. Grand Rapids, Michigan: Baker Academic.

Cox, M. (1998). "Description grammaticale du ncam (bassar)". Thèse de diplôme de l'École pratique des Hautes Etudes. École Pratique des Hautes Études.

Crunden, S (1984). "Initial study of prominence in Bassar Discourse". MA thesis. LBC-SIL (CNAA).

Daugherty, K (2007). "*Missio Dei*: The Trinity and Christian Missions". In: *Evangelical Review of Theology* 31.2, pp. 151–168.

Diprose, Ronald E. (2004). *Israël dans le développement de la pensée chrétienne*. Saône: La joie de l'Eternel.

Dobson, J (2005). *Learn New Testament Greek*. Grand Rapids, MI: Baker Academic.

Edgar, B (2004). *The Message of the Trinity*. Leicester: InterVarsity Press.

Gblem-Poidi, Massanvi Honorine (1995). "Description systématique de l'igo". Thèse de Doctorat Nouveau Régime. Grenoble: Université Stendhal.

Gblem-Poidi, Massanvi Honorine and Laré Kantchoa (2012). *Les Langues du Togo, Etat de la recherche, et Perspectives*. Paris: Harnatan.

Goldsmith, M (2002). *Good News for all nations: Mission at the heart of the New Testament*. London: Hodder and Stoughton.

Goucher, Candice (1985). "The Iron Industry of Bassar, Togo : An Interdisciplinary Investigation of African Technological History". PhD thesis. Los Angeles: University of California Los Angeles.

Gueu Nettaud, T. (2010). *Le Testament de Dieu pour les nations*. Abidjan: Edition Sel et Lumière.

Haley Barton, Ruth (2006a). *Sacred Rhythms: Arranging our Lives for Spiritual Transformation*. Leicester: IVP Books.

— (2006b). *Sacred Rhythms: Arranging our Lives for Spiritual Transformation*. Leicester: IVP Books.

Hiebert, G. Paul, Daniel R. Shaw, and T. Tiénou (1999). *Understanding Folk Religion*. Grand Rapids, MI: Baker Books.

Hoskins, B (1989). *Tout ce qu'ils veulent, c'est la vérité*. Nîmes: Vida.

Hunt, R (2010). *The Gospel among the nations: A documentary history of inculturation*. Maryknoll, NY: Orbis Books.

Jenkins, P. (2006). *The new faces of Christianity: believing the Bible in the global south*. Oxford University Press.

Jouon, Paul and T. Muraoka (1996). *A Grammar of Biblical Hebrew*. Rome: Pontificio Istituto Biblico.

Landes, M. G. (2001). *Building your Biblical Hebrew vocabulary*. Atlanta, GA: Society of Biblical Liberature.

Lenoir, F (2012). *La guérison du monde*. Paris: Arthème Fayard.

"Les langues au service du développement" (2004). In: *Le Traducteur: Bulletin d'échange de l'Association Wycliffe Togo* 1.

Myers, B. L. (1999). *Walking with the poor : principles and practices of transformational development*. Maryknoll, NY: Orbis Books.

Naveh, J. (1997). *Early History of the Alphabet*. Hebrew University, Jerusalem: Magnes Press.

Neill, S. (1964). *A History of Christian missions*. London: Penguin Books.

Pohor, R. and M. Kenmogne (2012). *Théologie et vie chrétienne en Afrique*. Wycliffe Global Alliance, Africa Area: ADG.

Pohor, Rubin and Michel Kenmogne, eds. (2012). *Théologie et Vie Chrétienne en Afrique*. Wycliffe Globale Alliance, Africa Area. Glô-Djigbé: ADG Editions.

Poidi, N (1987). "Phonématique et Système tonal su baassal. Une approche descriptive". Maîtrise. Paris III.

— (1995). "Etude Comparative du baasaal et de l'akaselem". Thèse de doctorat, Nouveau Régime. Université Stendal, Grenoble III.

— (2007). *What can we learn from a night of Seder in a Jewish Family?* Jerusalem: HBT.

Prost, André (1963). "Les classes nominales en bassari-tobote: comparaison avec le naoudem". In: *Journal of African Languages* 2.3, pp. 210–217.

Rendtorff, R. (2011). *Introduction à l'Ancien Testament*. Paris: Les éditions du Cerf / Verbum Bible.

Rosnay, Joël de (2012). *Surfer La Vie: Comment sur-vivre dans la société fluide*. Paris: Babel.

Sanneh, Lamin (1989). *Translating the message: The missionary impact on culture*. Maryknoll, NY: Orbis Books.

— (2003). *Whose Religion is Christianity? The Gospel beyond the West*. Grand Rapids, MI: William B. Eerdmans.

Saunders, P. (2004). *No Ordinary Book: A Bible Translator tells his story*. Belfast: Ambassador International Publications.

Smalley, W. (1991). *Translation as mission. Bible Translation in the modern missionary movement*. Macon, GA: Mercer University Press.

Smith, D.W. (2003). *Against the Stream: Christianity and Mission in an Age of Globalization*. Leicester: InterVarsity Press.

Stine, P. (2012). "Eugène A. Nida, Theoretician of Translation". In: *International Bulletin of Missionary Research* 36.1, pp. 38-39.

Stuart, D. (2001). *Old Testament Exegesis*. Louisville, KY: Westminster John Knox Press.

Swelmoe, W. (2008). *A new vision for missions: William Cameron Townsend, the Wycliffe Bible Translators and the culture of early evangelical faith missions*. Tuscaloosa, AL: The University of Alabama Press.

't Slot, Steef van (2000). *Évangélisation du monde: Que Tous Puissent Entendre*. WEC International, Afrique du Sud: Hebron Theological College.

Thomas, V. (2004). *Paper Boys: A vision for the contemporary church*. Milton Keynes: Authentic.

Townsend, William Cameron and S. Richard Pittman (1974, 1996). *Thou Shalt Remember All The Way*. Dallas, TX: Summer Institute of Linguistics, Inc.

Vaux, Roland de (1997). *Ancient Israel: Its Life and Institutions*. Grand Rapids, MI: Wm. B. Eerdmans Publishing.

Volf, M. (1998). *After Our Likeness: The Church as the Image of the Trinity*. Grand Rapids, MI: Wm. B. Eerdmans Publishing.

Walter, S. L., C. L. Jackson, and T. M. Lawson (1992). "GILLBT, 30 Years Ago". In: *Mother Tongue*.

Watkins, M. (1978). *Literacy, Bible Reading, and Church Growth Through the Ages*. Pasadena, CA: William Carey Library.

Wegner, P. (199). *The journey from texts to translations, The origin and development of the Bible*. Grand Rapids, MI: Baker Academic.

Westermann, Diedrich Hermann (1922). *Die Sprache der Guang in Togo auf der Goldküste und Fünf andere Togosprachen.* Berlin: D. Reimer (E. Vohsen).

Wilder, Charles K, ed. (1973). *Political Economy of Development and Underdevelopment.* New York, NY: Random House.

Winter, R. (1981). "The Concept of a Third Era in Missions". In: *Evangelical Missions Quarterly* 17, pp. 69–82.

— (2009). "Understanding the Polarization between Fundamentalist and Modernist Missions". In: *International Journal of Frontier Missions* 26.1.

Wright, Christopher J.H. (2006). *The Mission of God: Unlocking the Bible's Grand Narrative.* Nottingham: Inter-Varsity Press.

Wurthwen, E. (1995). *The Text of the Old Testament.* Grand Rapids, MI: Wm. B. Eerdmans Publishing.

www.ingramcontent.com/pod-product-compliance
Lightning Source LLC
Chambersburg PA
CBHW071503040426
42444CB00008B/1473